BUYER-APPROVED
Selling
Sales Strategies from the Buyer's Side of the Desk

BUYER-APPROVED
Selling

Sales Strategies from the Buyer's Side of the Desk

BY MICHAEL SCHELL

MARKETSHARE PUBLICATIONS

Buyer-Approved Selling:
Sales Strategies from the Buyer's Side of the Desk

Senior editors: Mitch Merker, Paul Goudie, Andy Fielding
Associate editors: Michelle Seidel, Arlene Prunkl, Patricia Anderson, PhD.

Published by Marketshare Publications Inc.
Suite 3030–700 West Georgia Street
Vancouver, British Columbia V7Y 1A1

Call us toll-free: 1-877-870-0009
Visit our website: www.marketsharepublications.com

First Printing, 2003

National Library of Canada Cataloguing in Publication Data
Schell, Michael, 1959-
Buyer-approved selling: sales strategies from the buyer's side of the desk / Michael Schell.

Includes bibliographical references and index.
ISBN 0-9731675-0-5

1. Selling. 2. Sales management. I. Title.
HF5438.25.S33 2003   658.85   C2003-910004-9
Cover Design by Jane Lightle
Interior Design by Andy Fielding

Printed in Canada

*In memory of my cousin
Andrew Douglas Schell
1969–2001*

Gratitude

g

It's great to have a dream, but it takes good people to help you make a dream a reality. This book is a reality because of the work of an incredible, inspiring team of friends and colleagues.

My good friend and fellow director of Marketshare Communications Inc., Jason Foyle, was directly responsible for setting up our book research facilities in Vancouver. My valued friend and business partner, Mitch Merker, provided incredible support, enthusiasm, mind-power, time, humor, and resilience. My good friend, Eva Nerelius, Business Operations Manager at Marketshare, spent many late night hours poring over charts and data. My friend Paul Goudie, General Manager of Marketshare, gave his passion, skill, and unwavering support.

My research team was relentless in their pursuit of the information this project required. Research coordinator Tanya Rauser spearheaded their efforts, spending countless hours contacting participants and organizing their responses. Researchers Clarice Abadilla, Vijay Anand, Jessica Andrews, Teresa Bailey, Mark Bourgeois, Joanna Bryniarska, Andrew Carson, Sean Cunningham, Shezmeen Hudani, Bianca Knop, Duncan Lea, Serena Lin, Jenna Lopez, Gordon Nesbitt, Don Roberts, Terri Rowson, Cassandra Stephens, and Frances Ubalde did an amazing job of cold-calling, interviewing, and collecting feedback from some of the busiest, hardest-to-reach decision-makers in North America.

My dedicated editorial team demanded excellence. Arlene Prunkl, Michelle Seidel, and Patricia Anderson, Ph.D., conducted the initial round of edits, followed by Mitch Merker, Paul Goudie and Andy Fielding. They always arrived early and stayed late to make this book happen. In particular, I appreciate Andy's simplification ideas; they helped us create concise material that sales professionals could use "right out of the box."

Jane Lightle, our cover designer, did an amazing job and took the time to get the look just right. Andy Fielding did an excellent job designing the charts and the book's interior, and carefully formatted the content. My uncle Joseph Schell took on the considerable task of compiling the chart data. Mark Savard made some valuable last-minute editing suggestions.

i

Christopher Locke of DaimlerChrysler, Greg Tennyson of Oracle Corporation, Mitch Bardwell of Canon USA, and Dane Christensen of the University of Phoenix generously allowed their endorsements to appear on the cover, and Christopher provided his excellent Foreword as well. Dr. Harry Hough, president of the American Purchasing Society, kindly promoted our project in his Professional Purchasing Newsletter.

Three insightful authors kindly allowed me to include excerpts from their books: Jill Konrath, Art Sobczak, and Bob Kantin.

Dr. Stephen Grant, Ph.D., and countless other friends and associates, reviewed this material at every stage of its development and gave it the benefit of their objective opinions and criticism.

Bill and Joyce Foyle provided much support, and an incredible atmosphere for writing, at their Raven's Pass.

The Panel of Professional Purchasers shared their knowledge, experience, and unique perspectives.

And finally, my mother Angela Hannaford and nephew Ben Schell motivated me to stay focused on this project and see it through.

To all of you, my sincere thanks!

Contents

Part 2: **Preparing**

Part 3: **Meeting**

Part 8: **Annoying**

Foreword

I am a buyer. In a typical day, I have numerous meetings with suppliers who hand me brochures and give overhead presentations designed to show me what their company can do for me. Rarely does a supplier ask me what I actually want.

I also have sales meetings with suppliers who can't understand why they rarely, if ever, get an order from me. They spend their time and energy criticizing the purchasing process, instead of focusing their time and energy on correcting previous mistakes and improving their prospects with me.

In both cases, I sit in my chair and gaze across the table at them, and think, "If I were a supplier, I know what I would do to satisfy my customer and increase future business."

That's what this book is all about: the *buyer's* point of view. It's about the lessons learned over years of requests-for-quotes, supplier lineup meetings, quote evaluations, negotiating, and purchase-order placement.

This book is an insight into the psyche of a buyer. It's an x-ray of the buyer's brain—of what the buyer is really thinking, but for political reasons may not articulate. It covers the buyer's goals, desires, and frustrations—from the smallest of supplier oversights to the largest of commercial blunders. It's the buyer's inner voice bellowing, "Hey you, what part of this commercial obligation don't you understand?"

This book gives professional sales reps a look into the world of the people who purchase from them. It gives them a chance to walk around in the buyer's shoes. It offers them a competitive edge and an opportunity for future growth.

This book gives the supplier the means to improve commerce, to improve profits, and most importantly, to improve relationships. My only wish is that suppliers read this book with a thirst to improve the way they do business, and thus reduce their vulnerability in the ever-changing market.

—Christopher Locke, Global Lead Buyer
DaimlerChrysler Corporation

Introduction

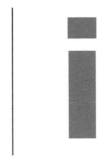

A few years ago, after twenty years in corporate sales, I decided to start my own company. Now it was my turn in the buyer's seat. With the tables turned and sales reps pitching to me, I realized how rare it was for reps to ask insightful questions. I also found that far too many reps hadn't prepared properly for their sales calls—I was amazed that they couldn't answer the most basic questions. They lost my respect because, as a buyer, I thought they showed not only lack of preparation but a lack of respect for my time. This made me question their accountability and reliability, and made me take my business elsewhere. Life is too short, and business is too important, to allow others to waste my time.

This shift in perspective, from sales professional to business owner, was like being hit on the head with a hammer. I realized clearly that the single biggest contributor to success in sales is to switch your focus from working *in* your job to working *on* your job. That is the difference that makes the difference.

Switching to the buyer's side of the desk has given me a greater appreciation of a sales rep's responsibilities. These include:

- Exploring and identifying needs
- Remembering details
- Honoring promises
- Confirming commitments
- Avoiding assumptions about a prospect's business
- Communicating with clarity

As a buyer, I like to deal with people who communicate concisely, knowledgeably, pro-actively, and dependably. I don't like to deal with people who waste my time, who make promises they don't keep, and who come to me only 60 percent prepared. I want 100 percent effort and ability from the people I *choose* to deal with.

As it relates to sales, the 80/20 principle means that 20 percent of sales professionals close 80 percent of the business. The other 80 percent of the reps fall into the "average" category and don't see the same results for their efforts. This means there is tremendous opportunity for the sales professional who wants to be a standout, a member of the elite class.

I saw the need for a book written from the perspective of experienced buyers who had met and interacted with countless sales reps over the years. Who better to help a sales professional to sell than a professional buyer?

For the purpose of this book, we can consider the decision-maker to be a prospect, a buyer, a purchaser, a procurement specialist, and so on. Consider that buyers may not always have the authority to say "yes" to a purchase decision, but they almost always have the authority to say "no."

This book is a practical guide and workbook for sales professionals and their managers. Effective selling requires you to differentiate yourself from the competition. Some of the tips and strategies in this book require extra planning and preparation, but when you're selling to your major accounts, you simply cannot afford to waste your opportunities. You must be at the top of your game. Remember, your competition wants the business too, and they are undoubtedly sending in their best people to close the deal.

So here it is at your fingertips—feedback from experienced, professional buyers. These corporate decision-makers have shared their opinions and advice on how to do your job better and win more of their business. Read the book, use the Planning Guides, and enjoy the success that comes from going the extra mile.

About this book

The Process

We made thousands of phone calls and interviewed hundreds of corporate sales trainers, sales reps, and sales managers from companies across the U.S. to gather the most effective sales strategies used in corporate America today.

We then presented these strategies to purchasing professionals from over 200 companies across America for their ratings and comments.

- Total number of buyers: **228**
- Total number of interviews: **330**
- Total questions presented: **4,327**

The Buyers

We were fortunate to have contributions from such a diverse and knowledgeable group of professional buyers. The buyers had an average of 17 years' experience, and many carried certifications including:

- Certified Purchasing Professional (CPP)
- Certified Professional Purchasing Manager (CPPM)
- Certified Purchasing Manager (C.P.M.)
- Accredited Purchasing Practitioner (A.P.P.)

Most of the buyers we approached received our book concept with enthusiasm. Even when buyers had to decline our invitation due to time constraints, they usually said, "It's about time somebody asked our opinions on the sales process." All of the buyers who contributed to this book were helpful and candid.

The Companies

We surveyed a variety of companies: Smaller firms with 50 to 100 employees; major corporations such as Daimler-Chrysler, Oracle Corporation, Sara Lee and Verizon with hundreds of thousands of employees; and companies in between. Industries included:

- Manufacturing
- Telecommunications
- Education
- Financial Services
- Aerospace
- Software
- Printing
- Health
- Hospitality
- Entertainment

Use of Buyer and Company Names

Where buyer names and company names appear with comments, we received permission to use them. Where comments are labeled *Anonymous* or no company names appear, consent was not available.

Prospecting

1

It all starts with a list: Organize and manage your prospect database for maximum results

You may already have a strategy for managing and prioritizing your territory's prospect database. If you don't, you may benefit by implementing this systematic approach to effective prospecting:

1. Compile or create your total prospect list.

2. Prioritize and number your list according to each prospect's potential.

3. From this master list, create a new list for each industry type. Since you have numbered your original list in the order of each prospect's potential, your new vertical market lists will also be in that order. Note: You can refer to these lists when creating your ISPS *(see pg. 4)*.

I get irritated when a rep truly does not understand the products they are selling and the applications of that product. This happens far too often for our liking. The problem seems to be that companies hire good salespeople but not good industry-specific people.

—Jim Morey, Vice President of Procurement
Sara Lee Foods, a division of Sara Lee Corporation

Develop an *Industry-Specific Positioning Statement* (ISPS) for each vertical market you target

Some companies have dedicated reps for customers in different vertical markets. The photocopier industry is a good example: The larger copier dealers often have reps who work only with lawyers, and others who sell only to accountants. These reps understand the ins and outs of the industry they serve. This presents a challenge for smaller dealers who don't have the resources to assign vertical-market specialists. They still try to sell to accountants and lawyers, but they're less successful because their approach is too general.

Be a specialist. Learn the vernacular of the industry. It's natural that people prefer to deal with experts who understand their specific industry's needs and challenges.

When you make that crucial first phone call, your ISPS can stimulate your prospect's interest and curiosity. It introduces you as an industry specialist and tells the prospect you can increase revenues or reduce costs.

ISPS Examples

- You are selling inventory-management software to the electronic manufacturing industry. A good ISPS could be: *"We specialize in lowering inventory management costs for electronics manufacturers."*

- Your targets are universities and colleges whose primary objective is to increase revenue through higher enrollment. A good ISPS could be: *"We're enrollment-creation specialists for the education industry."*

- You are selling corporate long distance services. Your ideal client makes a high quantity of calls under a minute in length, and their current provider bills in 1-minute increments. Because your company offers billing in 4-second increments, you can offer the prospect significant savings. A good ISPS for this call-center prospect could be: *"We specialize in reducing minimum billing costs for the call center industry."*

Planning Guide:

Creating
an ISPS

Step 1: *Using the prospect lists you made at the beginning of this book, create a list of specific companies you want to target:*

_____

_____

Step 2: *Identify and learn the industry vernacular while researching each company's website. Write down key words and phrases for potential use in your ISPS:*

_____

_____

_____

_____

_____

_____

_____

_____

Step 3: *Find out which associations serve the industry and write their names here. Research their websites and publications to understand the current state of that vertical market.*

_____

_____

_____

_____

Step 4: *Identify the key benefits your product or service offers this market.*

_____

_____

_____

_____

_____

_____

Step 5: **Write the ISPS.**

■ Try to limit your ISPS to 15 words. Remember, your objective is to quickly determine a potential fit with your prospect.

■ Emphasize how you can increase revenues or decrease expenses.

■ Become so familiar with your ISPS that it is second nature to you.

_____

_____

_____

_____

_____

_____

Comments from the Buyers

**Wm. Frank Quiett,
C.P.M., A.P.P.**

*Project Lead,
Supply Chain Management
and Strategic Sourcing*

"Excellent approach. The key here is to increase your knowledge, not to learn new buzzwords to sell with, but a real, honest-to-goodness knowledge base you can apply to the customer's industry-specific needs. Surface knowledge will get you in the door, but having a real working knowledge of the processes, requirements, and solutions will keep you there!"

Erik Schlichting

Inventory Control Manager

"There is nothing more irritating than someone who doesn't understand the pressures specific to my industry... This approach is an excellent way for a sales rep to learn about our business and be prepared."

Judy Elrite, C.P.M.

Buyer Specialist

"I get calls all the time and the salespeople seem to either patronize or fumble. If they knew what my company did and knew more about our industry, they would be smoother and much less annoying. I don't think I should have to teach them how to sell to my industry."

Peter Van der Hoek

Planner/Buyer

"If a rep could identify my industry type, our position in the market, and my company's needs, I would be impressed. I would feel more comfortable working with someone who has taken the time to learn about our industry."

Christopher Locke

*Global Lead Buyer
DaimlerChrysler Corp.*

"About 50 percent of my suppliers use this approach. The other 50 percent tend to focus on their company history and prior accomplishments rather than the benefits and opportunities for the client. They talk about their company instead of mine."

**Charles Tobler
C.P.M, M.P.P.**

Senior Buyer

"If this were done correctly, it would be a buyer's dream. It would be a great asset to understand our industry, and it would make it easier to explore mutual possibilities."

Grahame Gill
Facilities Buyer

"If a sales rep called me and used this approach effectively, there's a good chance he would get an appointment to meet with me."

✓

Tip 2b

In situations where an ISPS isn't appropriate, consider a *Primary Reason Statement* (PRS)

In some situations, an ISPS may not be appropriate or effective. For example, if your company had never sold to a particular industry, an ISPS wouldn't work. You couldn't validly claim experience in that particular field.

The PRS is a single sentence that identifies your line of business and tells your prospect the primary reason that companies do business with you. Simply structure your PRS by combining the word "specialists" or "specialize" with your company's main competitive advantage.

PRS Examples

- "We're a corporate long distance provider, and we specialize in reducing minimum billing costs."

- "We're a software company and we specialize in lowering inventory-management costs."

Tip 3

Create two *Key Point Statements* (KPS) for your Permission-Based Cold Call Guide

Key Point Statements deliver clear, concise information about your company/product/service—especially when you have limited time to get your point across and need to make a quick impact.

Two well-written KPS's that can be conveyed in 15 seconds or less can be very effective on the phone. Key Point Statements are not a sales presentation, so keep them brief.

To build KPS's:

1. List the four key points you want to make during the call.
2. Pair your key points to create two KPS's.

KPS Examples

A company that sells long distance services to businesses.

Step 1—identify four key points:

1. Your customers include Fortune 500 companies.
2. Your time is billed in 4-second increments.
3. You have the lowest per-minute rate in the country.
4. You're a stable, publicly-owned company.

Step 2—pair the key points to create two KPS's:

KPS 1: We've been around for 15 years, and we're a stable, publicly-owned company with a number of Fortune 500 clients.

KPS 2: You know, at three cents a minute, our corporate long-distance rates are the lowest in the country—and we bill in 4-second increments.

Planning Guide:

Key Point Statements

List the four key points you will use in your Key Point Statements:

1.

2.

3.

4.

Combine them to create your two Key Point Statements:

1.

2.

Tip 4

Do some basic research on your prospect companies before you call them

If you sort your prospects by industry type *(see pg. 3)* and create your ISPS *(see pg. 4)*, you should be ready to make intelligent initial calls to most of the people on your list. However, for your key prospects (where you may face more competition), you should prepare further by doing some more extensive research on those companies.

You may not always have time to research your key prospects as deeply as you would like. At minimum, try to find answers to these questions:

1. How many locations do they have, and is this the head office?
2. Has the company been in the news or had other publicity in the last six months?
3. Who are their major customers?
4. What are their main products and services?
5. What are their major industry challenges?

I prefer to be asked for a moment of my time, but only about 20 percent of sales reps ever do that.

—Lori Patten, Director of Projects–Development, Hyatt Hotels Corporation

Most of the reps who call on me don't ask permission for my time. When they do ask, and I don't have time, I usually show my appreciation by trying to schedule a future call.

—Tina M. Lowenthal, Associate Director, Purchasing Services, California Institute of Technology

Tip 5

Use a *Permission-Based model* for your cold calls

Your first call to your prospect has one goal: setting a qualified appointment. If you've completed the steps in Tips 1 through 3, it's simple to customize your own calling guide from Marketshare's permission-based cold call model.

Some conventional sales trainers think you should open cold calls by immediately delivering a key benefit, without first asking for a moment of the prospect's time. They believe that asking permission gives the prospect a chance to shut down the call before it begins.

However, could this lack of courtesy start you off on the wrong foot, and even make you seem invasive and annoying? The answer seems to be: Yes.

Marketshare Inc. has used a permission-based approach in over 150,000 cold calls. These calls were made to prospects in 33 cities across America, in a variety of industries including:

- Accounting
- Software
- Higher education
- Business associations
- Professional sports
- Financial services
- Office equipment
- Corporate training

An impressive eighty-five percent of the prospects responded favorably and agreed to proceed with the call. Of the remaining fifteen percent, the vast majority simply asked to be called again at a more convenient time. Using permission-based call models, Marketshare has set over 5000 appointments with busy decision-makers across America. These statistics indicate that you should feel confident using this model, regardless of your business type or location.

Planning Guide:

The Permission-Based Model

Use the model below to create your own Permission-Based guide for seeking appointments. This model assumes you have identified the decision-maker for your products or services.

Step 1: *Ask for permission to open the call*

"Hi, Monica, this is Cassandra from ABC Co. I don't need much time—do you have a quick minute?"

Step 2: *Present your ISPS or PRS*

"Thanks, Monica. We specialize in reducing minimum billing costs for the call-center industry."

Write your ISPS or PRS from Tip 2 here:

_____

_____

_____

_____

Step 3: *Determine the prospect's level of knowledge of your company, product or service*

"Are you familiar with / have you ever used / do you know much about..." [choose one]

- Our company?
- This process?
- This type of service?
- This product?
- This kind of application?

Step 4: *Using the ideas above, create your own question to determine the prospect's knowledge level:*

_____

_____

_____

_____

Step 5: *Ask for permission to present your Key Point Statements*

"Is it okay if I tell you a couple of key points about us / what we do / our product / this process?"

Write your own version of the question here:

_____

_____

_____

Step 6: *Present your two Key Point Statements*

- (example) "We're a stable, publicly-owned company with a number of Fortune 500 clients, and we've been in business for 15 years."

- (example) "We bill long-distance calls in 4-second increments, and at three cents a minute, our corporate long-distance rates are the lowest in the country."

Insert your Key Point Statements from Tip 3 here:

(1)

_____

_____

(2)

_____

_____

Step 7: *Ask your qualifying question*

"Monica, I have a quick question for you. Based on what I've told you so far, can you see any potential for ABC Co. to be of value to your business, either now or at some point down the road?"

Write your own qualifying question in the space below:

_____

_____

_____

_____

_____

Step 8: *Ask for the appointment*

"Monica, it would be great if I could stop by to see if we can help you out in any way. Are you available next Thursday? I won't waste your time."

(Prospect: "Yes, I'll be here.")

"Great, would 10:30 work for you?"

(Prospect: "No, I'm in meetings until noon.")

"Ok, how about 2 P.M.?"

Using the example as a guide, create your own question here:

_____

_____

_____

_____

_____

Step 9: *Confirm the appointment*

"Perfect. Just to confirm, then: I'll meet you at your office, 555 Vista Avenue, Suite 4000, on Thursday, November 14, at 2 P.M. Did I get that right?"

"Monica, can I leave my contact details with you? *[Leave your name and number.]* Thanks Monica, I'll see you next Thursday."

Permission-Based Cold Call: Supplement

When they don't have a "quick minute"

When you ask, "Do you have a 'quick minute?'," your prospect may say, "No, it's not a good time." Marketshare's experience suggests that this response is most effective:

"Is it okay if I give you a call back some other time?"

(Prospect: "Yes, that's fine.")

"Thanks—when would be the best time to call you back?"

When they just want information

One common response during a cold call is, "Can you just send me some information?" To effectively handle this question, consider these responses:

"Monica, I could send information, but in the interest of saving your time, how's this?: I've developed a Ten-Minute Meeting *(see pg. 21)* designed to identify our potential value to you—ten minutes and I'm out the door. I won't waste your time."

If prospect declines:

"Shall I email you a link to our website, or do you prefer printed information in the mail?"

(Prospect replies)

"Ok, I'll get that out to you today. Can I give you a quick call next Friday to see if a meeting makes sense for you then?"

Using voice mail to leave a message or sales pitch is meaningless without personal inter-action. People are tired of phone tag; make the effort to contact them personally.

—Wm. Frank Quiett, C.P.M., A.P.P.
Project Lead, Supply Chain Management and Strategic Sourcing

When making cold calls, don't clog the buyer's voice mail box with unsolicited messages

Imagine you're a buyer. How likely is it you'll have the time to return a continual barrage of unsolicited voice mail from sales reps you don't know, selling things you may not even need? Is that an effective way to initiate contact with a prospect? We asked the buyers: Should a rep you've never spoken to leave voice mail to make first contact?

Comments from the Buyers

Don Walraven
*Director of
Inventory Management,
Alaska Distributors Co.*

"No, I don't like voice mail for initial contact. Sales reps should try again until they get through."

Greg Adkins
Purchasing Manager

"It's better for a salesperson to keep calling until they get hold of me. It is in their best interest to do so, since in most cases I'm busy and may have to delete the message and move on."

Paula L. Martin
Corporate IT Buyer

"No, I very seldom return voice mail from reps who are prospecting. If I did that, I would be calling forty people a day. A better way: Call until I answer the phone."

Crystal Leonard
Buyer–Indirect

"I want reps to keep trying until they get me. Voice mail does not work with buyers. I have too much to do and cannot call people back when I have never talked to them before."

Carl Colasurdo
Director of Purchasing

"I don't suggest a rep leave voice mail for initial contact. Keep calling until I answer."

A 10-minute meeting is an ambitious objective. That promise may get you in the door— ONCE. To ensure you are on the road to building a partnership, you must accomplish what you have promised. You should work to stay on track, keep focused on the points you wish to make, and close your presentation with opportunities for cost-reduction. In today's economy, more and more buyers are operating under a cost-reduction charter from upper management. If you can help them achieve this goal, they will be more likely to listen and be open to further discussions.

—Lynne E. Gehrke, Vice President, Procurement
A.B.Dick Company

The Ten-Minute Meeting

Has this ever happened to you?:

You've done your homework on a prospect. You know they consistently use the type of product or service you provide, and you know who their current supplier is. You are confident that if you can set up a meeting you can earn some of their business. You make the cold call, but the prospect tells you she has no time to meet with you. It may be time to consider this approach:

"Monica, I know you're busy. I've prepared a ten-minute meeting agenda that will quickly determine if our company can be of value to you. When could we meet for ten minutes? I won't waste your time."

To prepare for an effective ten-minute meeting:

- Research the prospect's company.

- Define your meeting objective.

- Prepare intelligent, insightful questions.

- Rehearse your ten-minute power meeting with a colleague.

Comments from the Buyers

Yvonne Ventimiglia
Division Manager,
Leverage Purchasing,
Layne Christensen Company

"This approach shows respect for my time. Also, when a busy buyer is swamped with back-to-back meetings, this allows five or ten minutes in between to check phone messages, etc. It is not pleasant to be escorting someone out of the office while someone else waits."

Paula L. Martin
Corporate IT Buyer

"Time is valuable, so I think it's a great idea!"

Anonymous

"Most first meetings are too long. This approach sounds like it could be a timesaver."

Wendy Imamura,
C.P.M., CPPB, CMIR
Material Processing
Center Manager,
Verizon Hawaii Inc.

"Yes, I believe a power meeting can be a good door-opener."

If the interest was there, I would attend. All things being equal, this has the potential to influence my decision to a large degree. Properly executed, this type of activity could save a lot of wasted time.

—Richard K. Tyler, C.P.M., Director of Purchasing
MRC Bearings

Tip 8

Objective information-based seminars can be an effective prospecting tool

Position your company as experts in their industry by conducting practical, informative seminars. This can generate positive awareness among the companies you target and give your existing clients extra value.

The subject matter doesn't have to be entirely related to your product or service, but it must be of value to your target audience.

Ideas for an Effective Seminar

- Keep your seminar between 45 and 90 minutes.

- Provide objective, useful information. The seminar should not be a sales pitch.

- Set up a table at the back of the room with additional information such as brochures or content from the seminar. Make it available, but not mandatory.

- Following the presentation, give the participants a chance to interact. For some attendees, networking can be the most valuable part of the session.

- Provide a feedback form for attendees. Include sections for comments and ideas for future events.

- Mail each participant a letter thanking them for attending. If they provided feedback, consider referring to it in the letter.

Seminar Examples

- A security company hosts a seminar on workplace violence.

- A software company hosts a seminar on computer security.

We asked the Buyers: What percentage of reps offer informational seminars?

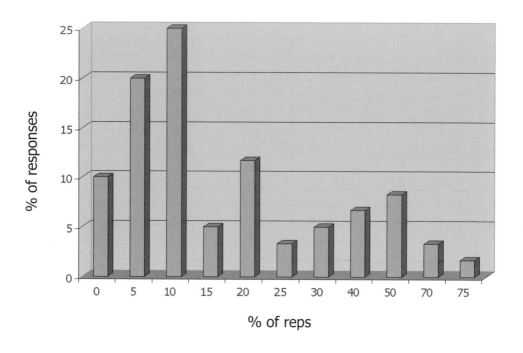

We asked the Buyers: On a scale of 0 to 10, how much do informational seminars influence your decision to buy?

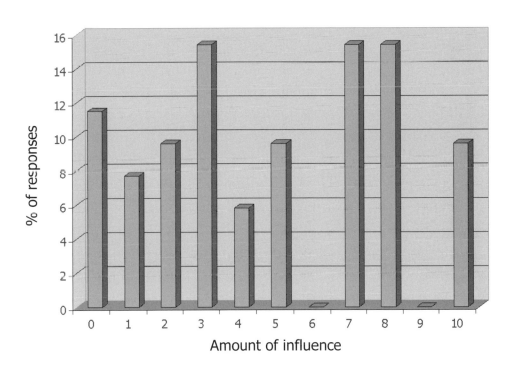

Comments from the Buyers

Kenneth F. Esbin
*Purchasing Manager,
Tarmac America*

"We're currently in the process of negotiating a very large contract with a number of potential suppliers. The deciding factors will be the ability of the selected vendor to share product knowledge and partner with us on appropriate industry strategies. Anybody can negotiate price, but I want a partner."

**Wendy Imamura,
C.P.M., CPPB, CMIR**
*Material Processing
Center Manager,
Verizon Hawaii Inc.*

"I'm familiar with these types of seminars. Chances are, if the seminar is truly objective and informative, that sales rep's company will be the first one we contact when looking for their type of product or service."

Kim Walker
*Facilities Manager,
Acordia Northwest Inc.*

"When it comes to deciding on a new vendor, all things being equal, if one of them conducted useful and informative seminars it would definitely help in influencing my decision."

Robert Click
Purchasing Manager

"This type of service would definitely influence my decision since it is meaningful and helps build a solid relationship with the vendor."

Errol van Edema
*Manager of Purchasing &
Manufacturing/Distribution*

"Purchasers like to be well-informed. A good supplier understands this and makes an effort to provide useful information resources to increase the value of the business relationship."

There's a really good chance I would read a postcard versus a letter. Postcards are easier to read and they quickly identify key points. I think this is a very effective method of direct mail.

—Henry Valiulus, Director of Purchasing

Tip 9

Supplement your follow-up with customized business postcards

Scenario: You have spoken with a prospect and determined they may need your product or service—not immediately, but sometime in the future.

While it's important to maintain contact, the buyers unanimously agreed that there was a fine line between keeping in touch with your prospects and annoying them. After three or four months of check-in calls, a call every month may stop being effective and become unwelcome.

This presents a dilemma for the sales rep:

- Excessive follow up: Annoy the buyer and lose the sale
- Not enough follow up: Be forgotten and lose the sale

In situations like this, a creative or humorous postcard can be valuable. When you use them to supplement your follow-up calls, you may increase your chances of getting business when the prospect is ready to buy.

Example: Follow-up Postcard

Marketshare needed a short-run printing of books, so we requested quotes from several suppliers. The proposals were followed up by calls, but by that time our plans had been delayed. All we could tell the reps was that we didn't know when we would need to run the job.

Four months later, we unexpectedly received an eye-catching postcard promoting short-run printing technology. It had a picture of a forlorn-looking author slumped at her desk, surrounded by thousands of copies of her new book. The caption read, "Why hasn't Oprah called?"

This card caught our attention—but more to the point, the timing was impeccable, as we were now ready to go to print.

To create your own business postcard, all you need is an idea that shows your product or service solving a problem—or, as with the card in the example, an idea showing the pain caused by *not* using your product or service.

You can also use postcards to communicate your Industry Specific Positioning Statement *(see pg. 4)*.

We asked the Buyers: What percentage of reps use postcards as marketing tools?

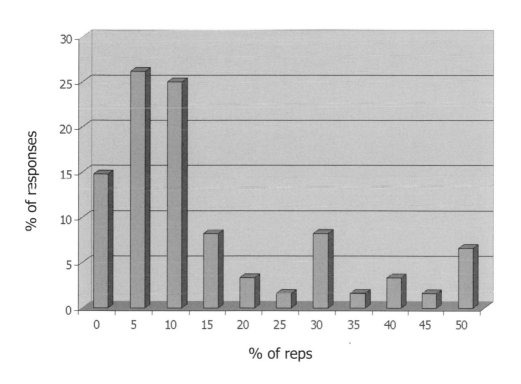

Comments from the Buyers

Richard Lusk

Director of Purchasing
Lennar Homes, Inc.

"I typically open all mail. A postcard has the potential to be more effective because it is a quicker read. I can make a decision about its worth much more quickly. A brochure and letter tend to take more time, and if the material contains an introduction, body, and closing, it may lose my attention. It must be brief so I can skim it."

Peter Van der Hoek

Buyer/Planner

"I would probably read a postcard, as they are usually more to the point. If it is of interest, then I would follow up and ask for more literature."

Charles Tobler
C.P.M., MPP

Senior Buyer

"I don't have time to read long sales letters. They just get a glance. The same goes for brochures, unless they catch my eye for an immediate need. There would, however, be about a 75 percent chance that I would read a postcard because they are small."

Kristen Mitchell

Senior Buyer
Boston Financial
Data Services Incorporated

"Give an eye-catching summary and only use 'target words' in the copy."

Wm. Frank Quiett,
C.P.M., A.P.P.

Project Lead,
Supply Chain Management
and Strategic Sourcing

"I receive flyers every day, and they just get pitched. The difference with a postcard is that I will give it a quick look."

Richard K. Tyler, C.P.M.

Director of Purchasing
MRC Bearings

"If it is not addressed directly to me it goes straight to the trash. Be sure the mailing is addressed specifically to the person you wish to reach. Items addressed 'Attn: Purchasing Dept.' or 'Attn: Purchasing Mgr.' probably won't reach anyone. Many mail-sorting departments have instructions to dispose of that type of mail."

Brad Bigelow

*Manager of Purchasing
and Vendor Relations*

"I would look at it if it were an interesting postcard. What I would really like to see is a postcard that incorporates a business card, with perforations to remove the card for future reference."

Preparing

2

Tip 1   Conduct appropriate research on your prospect's company before the meeting

Tip 2   Be ready to answer the toughest questions your prospect can ask

Tip 3   Use Genuine Preemptive Objection Statements (GPOS) in your sales meetings

Tip 4   Prior to each meeting, prepare a list of insightful questions to ask your prospect

Tip 5   Prepare a "page-at-a-glance" Company Information Sheet (CIS) customized for your prospect's industry

Tip 6   Prior to your meeting, email your prospect an Advance Meeting Agenda (AMA) and invite any changes to it

Credibility dissipates in front of your eyes. I won't trust their business and they won't get my business.

—Wayne Nordin C.P.M., V.P. & Procurement Manager
Sun Trust Bank

Tip 1

Conduct appropriate research on your prospect's company before the meeting

Don't waste your prospect's time with questions that can be answered by doing some homework. The sales professionals who win key accounts usually do extensive research before meeting with prospects. While buyers may not always notice that you have done this extra research, they sure notice when you haven't!

Here are some questions you may want to answer before the meeting:

- How many locations do they have, and is this the head office?

- Is the company private or public, and is there a parent company?

- Have they, or are they, acquiring any companies?

- Have they recently been in the news or had major publicity?

- Who are their competitors?

- Who are their major customers?

- What is their annual revenue?

- When is their fiscal year-end?

- What are their main product and service lines?

- Has anyone in senior management been replaced recently?

- Are they in a budget freeze?

- What are their major challenges?

To help with your research, try Internet search tools such as **www.copernic.com**. For publicly-traded companies, try **http://finance.yahoo.com** where you can find a company's financials, employee counts, officers' names, and website links.

We asked the Buyers: On a scale of 1 to 10, how important is it to you for a rep to do research prior to meeting with you?

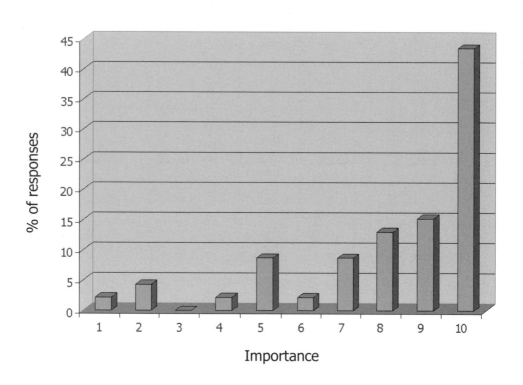

We asked the Buyers: What percentage of reps seem to have done their homework?

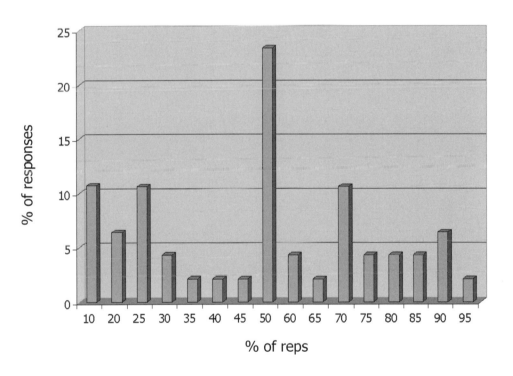

Comments from the Buyers

Sheryl Haeberle
Buyer
Brigham Young University,
Idaho

"I do not do business with someone who has not taken the time to learn about my business."

Judy Elrite, C.P.M.
Buyer Specialist

"It has an extremely negative impact. If they are not interested enough to do research, they are not interested enough to be doing business on a long-term basis. I have no wish to deal with lazy salespeople. How can they help me if they know nothing about my company?"

Mike Kanze,
MBA, C.P.M., A.P.P.
President
Cornerstone Services Inc.

"Big negative. They've wasted my time, as I've probably had to explain things they could have found out about us in the public domain."

Joyce M. Knapp, C.P.M.
Senior Buyer
Cooper Energy Services

"It gives me a negative impression. I think of them as not being good salespeople. I would not be as likely to have another meeting with them."

Jim Haining,
C.P.M., A.P.P., MBA
Manager, Corporate
Agreements, for a leading
telecommunications
company

"I generally turn them off quickly and terminate the meeting."

Can you give me some key performance indicators defined by your company—measures of success you've benchmarked against the industry to determine what you are doing well and what needs improvement?

—Greg Tennyson, C.P.M., CPCM, Vice President, Corporate Procurement
Oracle Corporation

Tip 2

Be ready to answer the toughest questions your prospect can ask

Many sales reps have great verbal agility—but the best ones take the time to be sure their answers will be the best they can be. There's nothing worse than being put on the spot with a tough question and having to struggle for an answer.

Examples: Tough Questions

- "I like your proposal, but the VP at our head office would make this decision. I'd like to promote it for you—how would you recommend I sell him on it?"

- "How can I be sure you'll honor your warranty?"

- "Let's say we're experiencing critical downtime with your product/service. How quickly can you get us up and running again? Can you give me an example of how you've handled this with other clients?"

- "Can you prove to us that your company is financially stable enough to honor your service warranty for the full term of the contract?"

Example Questions from the Buyers

Beckie Beard,
C.P.M, A.P.P, CACM

Director, Purchasing &
Materials Management
Lansing Community College

"What do you know about our needs for _____?"

"How long have you been selling this product/service?" [If less than a year:] "Do you really know enough about it that I should listen to your advice?"

Chris Nield

Corporate Buyer,
International Truck and
Engine Corp.

"What differentiates your product from your competitor's?" [I ask this of everyone in the first meeting.]

Wm. Frank Quiett,
C.P.M., A.P.P.

Project Lead,
Supply Chain Management
and Strategic Sourcing

"How can your company increase my effectiveness, reduce costs, or improve customer satisfaction?"

Grahame Gill

Facilities Buyer

"How can you help me save money?"

Jeff Hardman

Director of
Network Operations

"What is the value in your product/service?"

Mike Kanze,
C.P.M., A.P.P., MBA

President & CEO
Cornerstone Services Inc.

"Based on what you know about our firm, tell me why you think your product or service is right for us." [The answer to this question tells me a lot about how much the seller has looked at our business situation, and whether their offering meets a real need or is simply a "hammer looking for a nail."]

Dean R. Schlosser, Jr.

Purchasing Agent

"What differentiates your product from similar products?" [This moves the conversation toward issues such as support staff, service department, and price. This question is very good, especially if the same equipment is supplied by different companies under different names.]

Gregory W. Hunter
Manager of Purchasing
Cannon USA

"How can you improve my bottom line?"

Natalie Levy
V.P., Divisional
Merchandise Manager
Lord and Taylor

"Why do you think we will be successful if we choose your product?"

"Whom do you consider your competition?"

Steve Mataya
Materials Manager
Allied Gear &
Machine Co. Inc.

"What exactly will you do in terms of support and follow-through?"

"What competitive advantage can you provide me?"

Kenneth F. Esbin
Purchasing Manager
Tarmac America

"How is your company preparing for the potential strike in the _____ industry?"

"What do you see the economy doing? I know what my indicators say, but what do yours say?"

Planning Guide:

Tough Questions

Write some of the other tough questions you think your prospect could ask—and your answers.

Question:

_____

_____

Answer:

_____

_____

Question:

_____

_____

Answer:

_____

_____

Question:

_____

_____

Answer:

_____

_____

We asked the Buyers: What percentage of reps have trouble answering questions that you believe they should be prepared to answer?

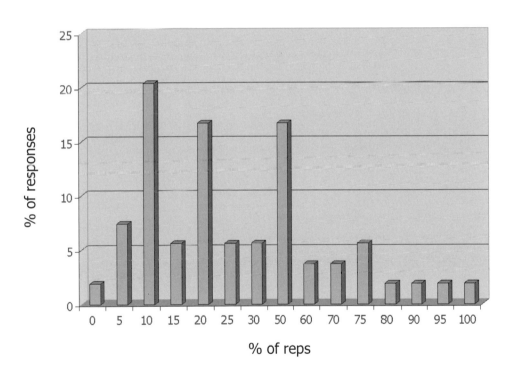

Key point for sales management

We asked the buyers if they had any favorite "tough" questions they liked to ask in the first meeting. The one that kept coming up was:

"Why is your company/product/service better than your competitors'?"

It is crucial to decide on the best way to answer this. Sales managers need to know: *Do all our sales reps answer this the same way? If not, who has the best answer? Shouldn't all of our reps be using that answer?*

One of the buyers, Peter Van der Hoek (Buyer/Planner) observed: "I find that some reps are baffled when you ask them what the advantages would be in dealing with them. You would think they were prepared for that type of question, but I am amazed how many are not."

It is rare for someone else to raise the objection first. It's unusual, but it's a very good idea.

—Brian Smith, Director of Inventory Management
Corporate Express

Tip 3

Use *Genuine Preemptive Objection Statements* (GPOS) in your sales meetings

Does this sound familiar?:

You're making a presentation, and it's going well—until your prospect raises an objection. Suddenly your carefully organized presentation has taken a 45-degree turn and you're on the defensive.

It doesn't have to be that way. When you can anticipate your prospect's objections and address them in a positive and informative way, you can actually give your prospect some key insights and enhance your presentation.

That's the power of the *Genuine Preemptive Objection Statement* (GPOS). We emphasize the word *genuine*—a GPOS works only when it is logical and forthright.

GPOS Examples

■ The conversation turns to price. You can introduce the following GPOS before your prospect brings up a lower-priced competitor:

"Yes, let's talk about price for a moment. Our product/service is priced about 20 percent higher than most of our competitors'—yet we're signing new business all the time. And in every case, the reason people buy from us is value. You see, independent research confirms our product's lifespan is nearly double the industry standard. So you get double the value, yet you pay only 20 percent more."

Notice how the rep cited his company's high standards without directly criticizing the competition. This is part of the "positive" in GPOS; it shows confidence and integrity.

■ You represent a small but fast-growing service provider. Your prospect has just complained about frequent service interruptions with their current provider. The prospect's next thought could be, "If XYZ MegaCorp can't give us dependable service, how can you?" This is a chance to use a GPOS. You can preempt the objection by explaining that your company's size allows it to specialize and give better service than a larger, diversified company:

"John, we're one of the smallest providers in the city, so it made sense for us to focus on a particular market niche and become experts in it. That's allowed us to deliver 23 percent more up-time than the local industry average."

Once you become familiar with the GPOS concept, you will realize there are regular opportunities to use them in prospect meetings. The key is to have your GPOS rehearsed and ready so you can notice when your conversation is heading for a likely objection. Remember, you're not responding to an objection, you're anticipating it. And even when your prospect objects before you can deliver your GPOS, you're ready to answer intelligently and positively.

Planning Guide:

Using the GPOS

Make a list of objections that commonly occur during your presentations. Choose the objections that could provide your customers with key information, and write a GPOS for each.

Potential objection:

_____

_____

_____

GPOS:

_____

_____

_____

Potential objection:

_____

_____

_____

GPOS:

_____

_____

_____

(more...)

Potential objection:

_____

_____

_____

GPOS:

_____

_____

_____

Potential objection:

_____

_____

_____

GPOS:

_____

_____

_____

We asked the Buyers: On a scale of 1 to 10, how effective do you think it is for reps to anticipate objections in a positive way?

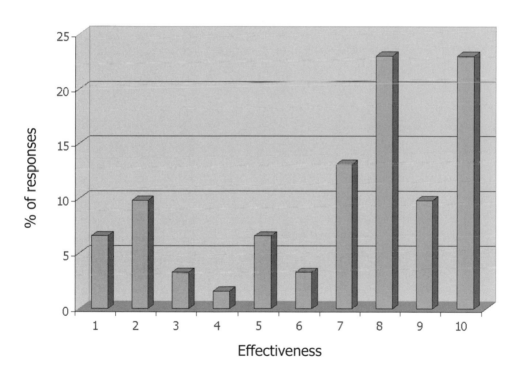

We asked the Buyers: What percentage of reps actually do this?

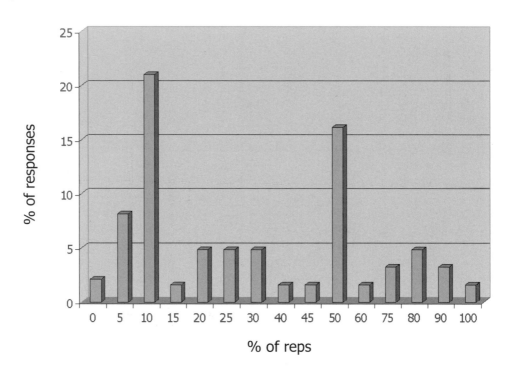

Comments from the Buyers

Edward DiLello, C.P.M.
Procurement Specialist
Philadelphia Gas Works

"This kind of proactive approach indicates to me that the rep knows his/her organization, its strengths and weaknesses."

Brent Long
Records Management
Coordinator

"This is a great idea, and it would save a lot of the beating around the bush that goes on regularly."

Wm. Frank Quiett
C.P.M., A.P.P.
Project Lead,
Supply Chain Management
and Strategic Sourcing

"Once a customer raises an issue, it becomes an objection. By bringing it up first, the sales rep keeps the customer from seeing it as a negative obstacle."

Stan Marshall, C.P.M.
Purchasing Manager

"It is always good to be proactive, and this definitely is."

Henry Valiulus
Director of Purchasing

"I think this a very good idea as long as it is done sincerely and doesn't bash the competition. Many reps are well-prepared to handle objections, but I've never experienced a rep presenting this in advance. It would save a lot of time."

Tip 4

Prior to each meeting, prepare a list of insightful questions to ask your prospect

Sales training resources suggest a wide range of questioning techniques:

- Probing questions
- Porcupine questions
- Objection questions
- Leading questions
- Third-party questions
- Comparative questions
- Developmental questions
- Presentation questions
- Motivation questions

There's a simpler approach. Compile a list of questions to help you achieve your *initial* sales meeting objective:

To quickly determine if your product/service can help your prospect's company increase revenues or decrease expenses.

We recommend you prepare for each sales meeting by creating a list of key questions specific to your prospect.

Examples: Key Questions

To help you create your own key questions, here are some ideas from two respected sales writers.

From *How to Sell More in Less Time With No Rejection, Using Common Sense Telephone Techniques (Volume 1)* by Art Sobczak

- What kind of turnaround time do you really want, and what do you get now?
- How do you measure good service?
- How would you define a good value for your money?
- What was the criteria you used when you chose your present supplier?
- What were the determining factors in selecting the company you're now using?
- If you could design the perfect _____, what would it look like / do?

Consider starting questions with phrases such as:

- When was the last time you needed to...?
- What do you do when...?
- How would you handle...?
- What happens when...?

Our thanks to Art Sobczak for allowing us to include this important material. You can reach Art at:

Business By Phone Inc.
13254 Stevens St.
Omaha, NE 68137
1-402-895-9399
www.businessbyphone.com

From *Winning More Sales: Take Your Business to the Next Level with Insightful, Powerful Questions* by Jill Konrath

- From a _____ perspective, what are the biggest challenges your firm is facing today?
- What things are most important to your customers today?
- What are the greatest challenges your department faces in achieving its objectives?
- How do your problems with _____ prevent you from achieving your objectives?
- What's the Ripple Effect of the problem you described? What other areas are impacted?
- How do you measure success working with your current supplier?
- What are your criteria for establishing a new business relationship?
- If you determine that several companies meet your needs, what other criteria become important in your decision?
- Are you aware of any obstacles to us working together on this project?

Our thanks to Jill Konrath for allowing us to include this important material. You can reach Jill at:

Selling to Big Companies
2227 Foxtail Court
White Bear Lake, MN 55110
1-651-429-1922
www.sellingtobigcompanies.com

Example Questions from the Buyers

Trent N. Baker, C.P.M.
Purchasing Manager
Wilson Foods, Division of
Reser's Fine Foods, Inc.

"What's the most important thing a supplier like us could do to help you and your company be more effective and profitable?"

Scott Bartel
Sourcing Strategist

"What do I need to do to help you compare your present vendor's offering versus mine?"

Lori Aljets
Purchasing and Quality
Assurance Manager
Norpac Foods Inc.

"I want to exceed your expectations. How would you go about defining a good supplier?"

Grahame Gill
Facilities Buyer

"What do you look for when selecting a product or service?"

We asked the Buyers: What percentage of reps ask you good questions on their sales calls?

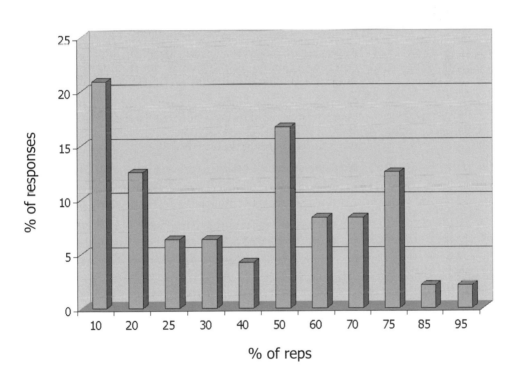

This is a ten out of ten. Most sales reps spend 15 minutes of my time going over brochures and talking about their company whether I know about them or not. I really like the idea of a single-page synopsis of company information.

—Anne Stilwell, Director, Contract and Procurement Services
Fannie Mae

Tip 5

Prepare a "page-at-a-glance" *Company Information Sheet* (CIS) customized for your prospect's industry

Our research shows that when it comes to presenting initial information on a sales call, "less is more."

Buyers often receive pages and pages of information they don't have time to read. If they're not reading your printed information, does it matter how impressive it looks?

Instead, prepare a concise Company Information Sheet for your prospect, containing a bulleted list with these items:

- Your ISPS *(see pg. 4)* or your PRS *(see pg. 9)*
- Your years in business
- An example of how your company gave ROI to a client in the prospect's industry
- A list of some current clients—ideally, 12 clients in the prospect's industry *(see pg. 80)*
- Any relevant company certifications or awards

Planning Guide:

Company Information Sheet

Use this page to plan your own Company Information Sheet.

Your ISPS (see pg. 4) or PRS (see pg. 9):

_____

_____

_____

Your years in business:

_____

How your company gave ROI to a client in the prospect's industry:

_____

_____

_____

_____

A list of some current clients—ideally, 12 clients in the prospect's industry (see pg. 80):

_____

_____

_____

_____

_____

_____

_____

_____

_____

_____

_____

Relevant company certifications or awards:

_____

_____

_____

_____

_____

Comments from the Buyers

Gene Roberts
Manager of Purchasing

"Most reps send pages and pages of information about their company, and I don't have time for that. If they're doing a cold call or trying to introduce their company, they should have the one-page summary. They should all be using this approach, but I've never met one who did."

Leslie Champion
Senior Procurement Specialist, Industrial Design & Construction, Inc.

"It's a good idea. Short bullet points and a single page are more likely to be read than pages of data about your company."

Roy Sekigawa
Purchasing Operations Manager, Foremost Dairies, Hawaii

"I first saw one last week. It's useful for comments and feedback as well. Only a small percentage of reps use this type of sales tool, and I'd like to see more of them. I'd give this a nine out of ten."

Wendy Imamura, C.P.M., CPPB, CMIR
Material Processing Center Manager, Verizon Hawaii Inc.

"I think a company information sheet is helpful. Take care to ensure that information is constantly updated. It is not worthwhile to spend a lot on glossy printing and volume, since dated material looks worse than no material!"

Jason Wihnon
Supply Purchaser IKON–IMS

"This is a nine out of ten since it would be a valuable sales aid. In ten years of purchasing I haven't seen one, but it's a great idea."

Angel Tutor
Purchasing Coordinator Wackenhut

"I think this is an excellent idea that very few reps use. I like this a lot."

"It is easier to set up the attendee list when you have an agenda. It also allows for adding to the agenda or removing what you don't want. At my company, no one has time to spend on meetings that do not specifically address their needs. "

—Toni Horn, C.P.M.
Global Commodity Manager, Silicon Graphics Inc.

Tip 6

Prior to your meeting, email your prospect an *Advance Meeting Agenda* (AMA) and invite any changes to it

An agenda is a prerequisite for all sales meetings. It should chronologically list your sales meeting's key topics. When you email your prospect an Advance Meeting Agenda, you:

- Show respect for the prospect's time and your interest in addressing the company's needs

- Learn more about the company's needs and are able to prepare for them

- Let the prospect feel more involved in the meeting process

- Let the prospect prepare any required information

- Show you have done your "homework" researching the company

- Show that you are organized and competent

**Example:
Advance Meeting
Agenda**

On the next page is an example of an email message introducing an AMA. (In the example, *BuyerCo* is the buyer's company; *ABC Co.* is the sales rep's company.)

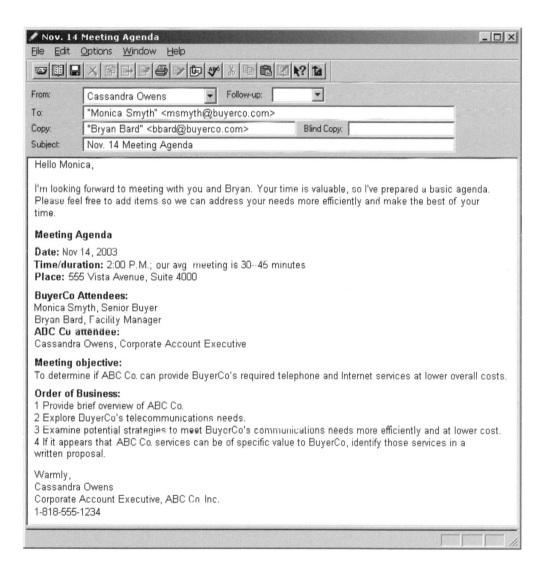

Example: Advance Meeting Agenda

We asked the Buyers: On a scale of 1-10, how important is it for reps to prepare a meeting agenda in advance?

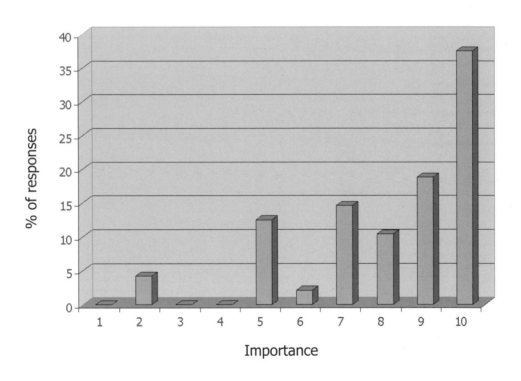

Comments from the Buyers

Wm. Frank Quiett
C.P.M., A.P.P.
Project Lead,
Supply Chain Management
and Strategic Sourcing

"The proposed agenda gives the buyer or manager something with which to compare his requirements and interest, and allows him to share the agenda with colleagues, management, and cross-functional teams. Also—and this is important—it gives him or her the opportunity to adjust the meeting to meet a specific interest prior to the meeting. Actually, I would recommend that the letter ask the buyer to respond with 'Yes, this is fine,' or 'I would like to recommend...' Either way, you are getting 'buy-in' up-front and putting substance into the meeting."

Natalie Levy
V.P. Divisional
Merchandise Manager
Lord and Taylor

"I think it's great to know what the topics will be before the meeting. It shows that the sales rep is serious and prepared for the meeting."

Stan Marshall, C.P.M.
Purchasing Manager

"It helps define the time period that will be needed for the meeting and the areas which have to be covered. If there is no need to cover a particular area due to current agreements, this reduces the waste of our time."

Lori Aljets
Purchasing and Quality
Assurance Manager
Norpac Foods Inc.

"It suggests an organized, educated, interested company."

Richard Lusk
Director of Purchasing
Lennar Homes, Inc.

"It would cut to the chase and prepare the participants for a direct and pointed meeting."

Mike Kanze,
C.P.M., A.P.P., MBA
President & CEO
Cornerstone Services Inc.

"Presented sufficiently in advance, it gives the buyer the opportunity to reject inappropriate agenda points or change them accordingly. It also forces the vendor to think rationally in advance about the meeting and to set realistic goals about the meeting's outcome."

Lynda Stewart
General Manager
Praga Industries Co. Ltd.

"It verifies and confirms the appointment and gives the buyer an opportunity to prepare the required information and make changes."

Jim Morey
Vice President–Procurement,
Sara Lee Foods, a division of
Sara Lee Corporation

"This is pretty important. It helps to keep you on track in the meeting, and it makes things much more efficient."

Dusty Rhoads, C.P.M.
Contract Administrator
First Energy Corporation

"It's important—a ten out of ten—but only if the rep has done their homework and the agenda contains relevant, to-the-point bullets."

Christopher Locke
Global Lead Buyer
DaimlerChrysler Corp.

"Unfortunately, only about 10 percent of my suppliers follow this procedure. If I could receive an agenda prior to the meeting and remove or add any content that would not be advantageous to me, it would certainly help the supplier, who could then spend more time on issues of interest to me."

Key point for sales management

When two or more company representatives team up for a sales meeting, it is important for them to plan and rehearse their presentation to ensure seamless, professional delivery.

Planning Guide:

Teaming Up

Use this space to plan how you and your colleagues will handle these important aspects of a team presentation:

How will the agenda items be divided?

_____

_____

_____

_____

_____

_____

_____

_____

Who will answer questions about service, price, warranty, and other specific topics?

_____

_____

_____

_____

_____

Who will answer any unanticipated or sensitive questions?

_____

_____

Comments from the Buyers

Ronald D. Ewen
*Purchasing Agent &
Assistant Projects Manager*

"Usually, when meeting with two reps from the selling company, one is a superior of the other—like a sales manager and a sales rep. One tends to be more dominating—usually the sales manager—and the other, more intimidated by the situation. They don't act as a team at all. In my experience, this happens 100 percent of the time."

Anonymous

"When two representatives meet with me, they sometimes interrupt each other when answering my questions, or they have conflicting answers. This does not instill confidence in the buyer."

We asked the Buyers: What percentage of rep teams are clearly unprepared when they meet with you?

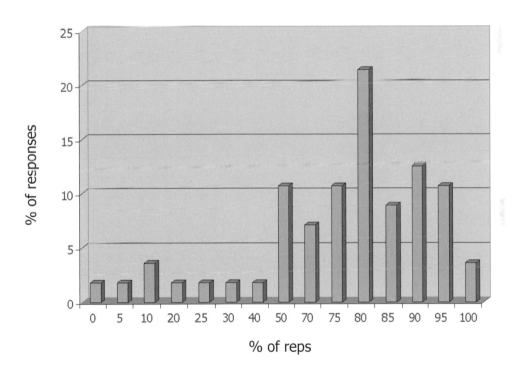

Meeting

3

Tip 1   Before you ask the prospect about their business, establish your credibility by giving your prospect a brief overview of your company

Tip 2   Prepare a Meeting Planner as a guide for your sales meetings

Tip 3   Leave your prospect with some objective questions that could be critical to the purchasing decision

Tip 4   Give your prospect a list of your clients specific to their industry and invite the prospect to contact three of them for references

Tip 5   After you answer a complex question, confirm that you've answered it to the buyer's complete satisfaction

Tip 6   At the close of the meeting, summarize the key points you discussed

It makes sense for sales reps to start off with a brief introduction of their company. I can't tell them what my needs are until I know what they can offer.

—Brian Moran, Director Americas, Supply Management
Siemens Westinghouse Power Corporation

Tip 1

Before you ask the prospect about their business, establish your credibility by giving your prospect a brief overview of your company

It's important to map out your sales-meeting strategy, but pay close attention to respect and courtesy. For example, earn the right to ask your prospect questions by first establishing your credibility. The idea is not to sell, but to give the buyer enough information to make them comfortable about continuing the conversation. We recommend the following approach:

■ State your ISPS *(see pg. 4)* or PRS *(see pg. 9)*.

■ Name a few of your key accounts.

■ Using the example from your Company Information Sheet, briefly describe how your company provided ROI to a client in the prospect's industry.

■ Give the prospect a printed copy of your Company Information Sheet *(see pg. 56)*.

Example: Company Overview

"Monica, before we get into the meeting, I was hoping I could share a few key points about [my company]. Would that be ok?"

[Sales rep continues:] "We specialize in reducing minimum billing costs for the call-center industry. We've worked with XYZ Call Co and CBD Calling for You Co, two of the largest centers in the US. In fact, XYZ Call Co selected us out of five vendors, and we've been saving them 30 percent a month ever since. May I leave this company information sheet with you? Great. Now may I ask you a few questions about [your company]?"

Tip 2

Prepare a *Meeting Planner* as a guide for your sales meetings

You have finally connected with an elusive key prospect. You asked the right questions, said the right things, and you got the appointment. The prospect made it clear you were the last of five suppliers he was considering. But you've done your homework, and you've prepared your meeting planner—a tool designed to ensure that your meeting goes smoothly and effectively.

Meeting Planner Components

The meeting planner is a binder or folder that organizes the items you need for a successful meeting: A checklist and appropriate supporting documents, all of which are covered in this book.

Planning Guide:

Meeting Planner

Use this checklist to help you assemble your own Meeting Planner. Each item is preceded by the page number where it is described. A Document Checklist is included at the end.

Page 60	_____	Advance Meeting Agenda (AMA)
Page 71	_____	Company overview
Page 56	_____	Company Information Sheet (CIS)
Page 52	_____	Questions
	_____	Proposal required?
Page 80	_____	References
Page 87	_____	Summary of key points and action items
Page 128	_____	Post meeting: send email summary
Page 91	_____	Prepare proposal

(more...)

DOCUMENT CHECKLIST:

Page 60   _____ Advance Meeting Agenda (AMA)

Page 56   _____ Company Information Sheet (CIS)

Page 52   _____ Question sheet

Page 39   _____ Answers to potential questions

Page 35   _____ Company research sheet

Page 75   _____ Critical questions sheet

We asked the Buyers: What percentage of reps are clearly unprepared for the sales call and have apparently not planned a meeting structure?

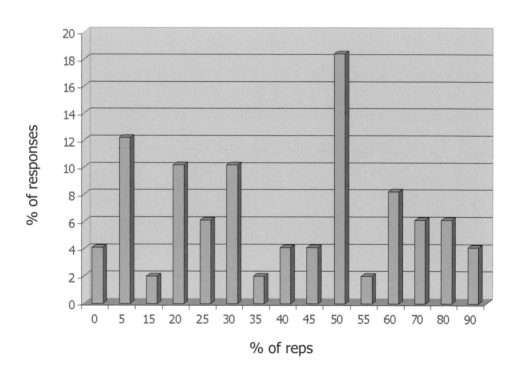

Implying that they understand your problems and have the willingness to answer questions about their competitors shows confidence in their company, products, and their ability to understand the industry. That is very important to me.

—David Mizer, Vice President Strategic Sourcing
Carnival Cruise Lines Inc.

Leave your prospect with some objective questions that could be critical to the purchasing decision

Toward the close of the meeting, give the buyer a list of objective questions to ask any vendor before making a final decision. By providing some important questions the buyer might not have considered, you can help the buyer make a better decision.

At the end of the sales meeting, you can introduce your list of questions this way:

"Monica, I've put together a few questions that may be helpful in making your decision. They're objective questions that you should ask any vendor before you decide to move forward. May I leave them with you?"

**Examples:
Questions
for Vendors**

- What happens if you can't honor your service response-time guarantee?

- What happens if replacement parts are discontinued?

- What contingency plan do you have for service interruptions?

- Do you have tracking reports I can access online?

- What happens if we have an equipment failure? Does your company provide a loaner? If so, does it cost anything?

- When you service our equipment, do you use new or refurbished parts?

- Do you recycle your discarded parts? Do you have other environmental policies?

Planning Guide:

Questions for Vendors

Create your own list of objective questions critical to the buyer's decision:

_____

_____

_____

_____

_____

_____

_____

_____

_____

_____

_____

_____

_____

_____

_____

Comments from the Buyers

Greg Graham
Buyer
Kenworth Truck Company

"Interesting idea—I've never seen anyone do it. I think the questions would have to be objective in order for it to be effective."

Kristen Mitchell
Senior Buyer
Boston Financial
Data Services Incorporated

"This could be very helpful, but be careful not to put down competitors in an effort to make your company look better. The right questions should be indicators that the seller has confidence that his/her company has the preferred response."

Lynda Stewart
General Manager
Praga Industries Co Ltd

"If these questions were made available, I think they would have some value in the decision making process."

Richard Lusk
Director of Purchasing
Lennar Homes, Inc.

"Maybe they will bring up something we haven't considered. That would be helpful for us."

Edward DiLello, C.P.M.
Procurement Specialist
Philadelphia Gas Works

"This would be valuable because different reps bring different experiences and perspectives to the table. Situations may have occurred elsewhere that have not occurred (yet) in the buyer's organization."

We asked the Buyers: At the end of a sales meeting, if a rep left you with two or three objective questions to ask other vendors—questions that would help you make the best buying decision—how valuable would that be on a scale of 1 to 10?

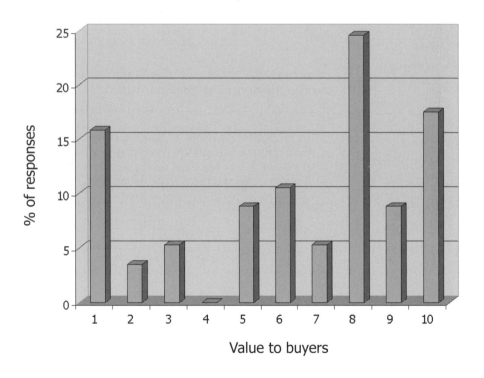

We asked the Buyers: How many reps do this?

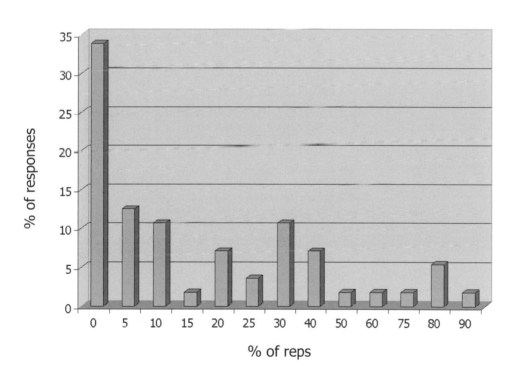

A testimonial letter on its own rates a two out of ten. The value of references we can call are a ten out of ten.

—Jim Morey, Vice President–Procurement
Sara Lee Foods, a division of Sara Lee Corporation

Tip 4

Give your prospect a list of industry-specific clients and invite the prospect to contact three of them for references

It's a common belief that glowing testimonial letters can influence a sale. But think about it: Have you ever read a *bad* testimonial? How useful are they as a sales tool?

When we interviewed the buyers, we found they valued testimonial letters much less than they did appropriate references with whom they could speak directly. In general:

- Buyers felt that testimonial letters had little or no impact on their decisions.

- Buyers felt that good, live references had significant influence on their decisions.

Scenario: Client References

You're in an initial sales meeting. You've determined there is a fit, and the prospect has asked you to prepare a proposal. As you are summarizing the requirements for the proposal, you offer the prospect the opportunity to call three of the clients on your Company Information Sheet *(see pg. 56)*. You invite them to select any three clients, and tell them you will include the contact information for these references in your proposal.

For each client on your reference page, include:

- The references' contact information

- Their products and services

- The number of years they have been your client

- A brief description of how your reference benefited from doing business with you

Comments from the Buyers

Toni Horn, C.P.M.
Global Commodity Mgr.
Silicon Graphics Inc.

"Testimonial letters or awards from other customers alone do not impress me. The above approach would be very effective in gaining my business."

David Frieder
Purchasing Director
Planet Automotive Group Inc.

"I would want references from people who are in my field and who have related needs. I'm not interested in a reference from someone whose needs are different from mine."

Jim Haining, C.P.M., A.P.P., MBA
Manager, Corporate Agreements, for a leading telecommunications company

"Forget the testimonial letters and give me references that I can call and question directly."

Judy Elrite, C.P.M.
Buyer Specialist

"I much prefer talking to references and asking them questions directly. They need to be references that have something in common with my company or industry."

Erik Schlichting
Inventory Control Manager

"If I cannot call and confirm a current level of satisfaction, they mean almost nothing."

Richard Lusk
Director of Purchasing
Lennar Homes, Inc.

"I always ask for references when going through the vendor selection process. Testimonials with call info would be well-received."

Michael Tator
V.P., Director of Production, Wunderman, of the Y&R Companies, Irvine

"I require the option of being able to telephone past clients—which I do follow up on. There are always production-related questions I need to ask that are not covered in the letters and testimonials."

Carl Colasurdo
Director of Purchasing

"I have yet to receive a testimonial or letter of recommendation that made me want to deal with a specific vendor. I would probably be more impressed if I were handed a binder of letters from past customers that complained about the lousy service and high prices that the vendor provided—and if the representative then explained how the company resolved those issues and moved to a higher level through this customer criticism. Getting all the happy guys to write letters is of little value."

It is very important for the rep to make sure he has answered the question completely. Otherwise, it could cause expensive problems in the future—for both of us.

—Paula L. Martin, Corporate IT Buyer

Tip 5

After you answer a complex question, confirm that you've answered it to the buyer's complete satisfaction

Assume responsibility for clear communications by making sure that you've properly answered complex questions. In the natural flow of conversation, it is easy to move past one issue and jump into the next without any guarantee that both parties are "on the same page." Instead, confirm that your prospect understands by asking:

"Did I explain that clearly enough?"

Do *not* ask, "Did you get that okay?"

Example: Confirming Your Response

Prospect: "I'm concerned about having users in different locations accessing the network. We have seven locations, and each location has twelve stations. Taking into account our need for maximum reliability and uptime, my question is, 'How many users per location can access the network and how many total locations can we integrate?'"

Sales Rep: "Our reliability is 100 percent guaranteed. Over 5000 clients are using our service, and none has ever had less than 98 percent uptime. Also, with our advanced system, up to 200 users can simultaneously access the network from up to ten remote locations. Each location allows a maximum of 20 users."

[Sales rep continues:] "Monica, I just want to make sure I understood your question. Did I explain that clearly enough?"

We asked the Buyers: On a scale of 0 to 10, how important is it to you for a rep to confirm replies to your complex question?

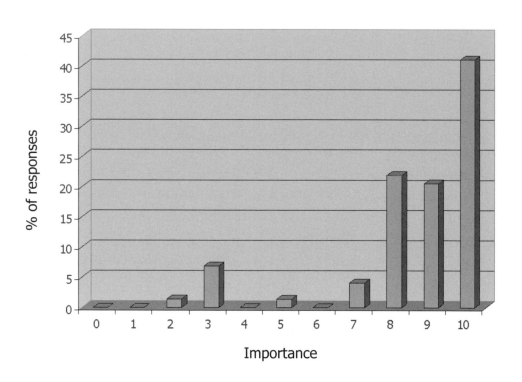

We asked the Buyers: What percentage of reps actually do this?

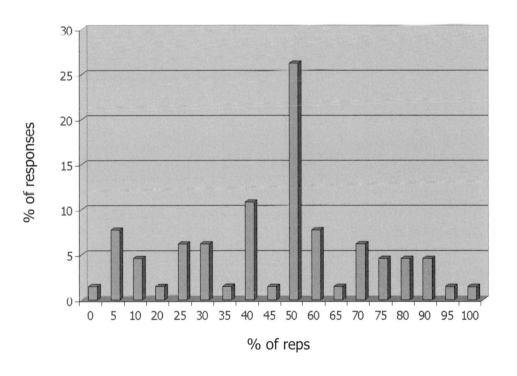

Comments from the Buyers

Don Walraven
*Director of Inventory
Management
Alaska Distributors Co.*

"This makes sense. It's important to make sure that both sides fully understand what is being said or agreed."

Sheryl Haeberle
*Buyer,
Brigham Young University
Idaho*

"It is extremely important to confirm understanding when the questions are complex."

Joe Hoffman
Commodity Manager III

"It is extremely important that reps check to see if they handled questions properly."

**Wendy Imamura,
C.P.M., CPPB, CMIR**
*Material Processing
Center Manager
Verizon Hawaii Inc.*

"Confirmation questions should be asked by the salesperson just in case the prospect is not comfortable about asking the same question over and over. The salesperson should also be trained in giving multiple examples to stress a point."

**Wm. Frank Quiett
C.P.M., A.P.P.**
*Project Lead,
Supply Chain Management
and Strategic Sourcing*

"Making sure that questions are clearly understood is critical to the continuing relationship the rep and the customer are trying to build."

Errol van Edema
*Manager of Purchasing &
Manufacturing/Distribution*

"Quality of information is paramount in the purchaser's work. Purchasers rely on the information provided by the reps, and that information flows to our internal customers. The rep's information and accuracy reflects on the buying organization."

When you conclude a meeting, it makes sense to confirm the key points discussed. It's important that all parties are confident that real communication has taken place. A concise summary is an ideal way to achieve this goal.

—Andrew Jules DeGiulio, Purchasing Manager

Tip 6

At the close of the meeting, summarize the key points you discussed

At the close of the meeting, summarize the key points you discussed to ensure that you and your prospect understand one another completely.

Example: Summarizing Key Points

"Monica, if I can just recap the key points of our meeting: Tomorrow, I'm going to call Tracy Jackson to find out how much of your monthly long distance is affected by the current 1-minute minimum. I'll put together a written comparison which will compare what you're currently paying with our 4-second minimum billing format.

"Then on Thursday I will meet with Kevin Lee, your operations manager, at the branch office in Richmond and conduct the same review I did with Tracy.

"And by Friday at 3 P.M., I'll have a proposal at your office.

"Does that cover everything, or is there anything I might have missed?"

We asked the Buyers: What percentage of reps summarize the key points you discussed during your meeting?

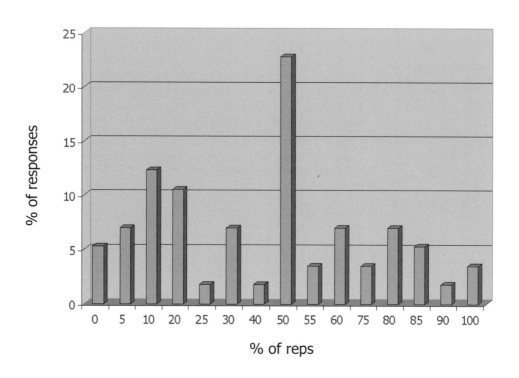

We asked the Buyers: On a scale of 1 to 10, how valuable is it to you when a rep summarizes the key points of your meeting?

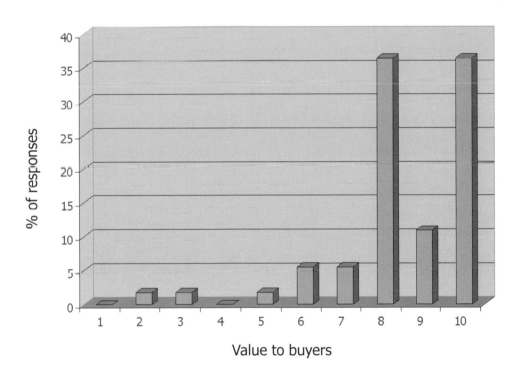

Comments from the Buyers

Lynne E. Gehrke
*Vice President,
Procurement
A.B.Dick Company*

"Summarizing at the end of a meeting has great value. If I were to do sales training, this is one of the top skills I would definitely teach. It keeps both sides on track and becomes a very effective tool when confirmed via email. I use it today as an action item checklist."

Natalie Levy
*V.P. / Divisional
Merchandise Manager
Lord and Taylor*

"This summarizing step is necessary so all parties are clear on how to proceed."

Stacey J. Zetterlund
*Supervisor, Direct Material
Sourcing, MRC Bearings*

"If the rep doesn't summarize the key points and list the action items, then I do."

**Mike Kanze,
C.P.M., A.P.P., MBA**
*President & CEO
Cornerstone Services Inc.*

"This is an important step. Often, I'm the one who summarizes because the rep forgets."

Kenneth F. Esbin
*Purchasing Manager
Tarmac America*

"Only about five to ten percent of the people I meet with actually make sure that we've communicated clearly on all points. It's important to summarize what was discussed and identify what the next steps are."

Peggy Jones
*Operations / H.R. Director
Magic Software Enterprises,
Inc.*

"Summarizing key points gives me a chance to confirm expectations from the meeting and allows me to respond with any additions or changes I might have."

Proposing

4

The proposal is important when determining which vendors should be short-listed. When certain buying decisions are shared, a properly detailed proposal is valuable because it addresses the concerns of all the departments involved.

—Dean R. Schlosser, Jr., Purchasing Agent

For more complex sales, consider a *Strategic Proposal*

Your planning and preparation paid off with a well-orchestrated meeting. You asked the right questions, said the right things, and confirmed an opportunity to help the buyer increase revenues. Your prospect has requested a proposal—you're on the shortlist.

When it comes to creating proposals, many companies use preset formats that suit most selling situations. For more complex sales, consider a strategic proposal.

We are fortunate to have the contribution of a recognized expert in sales proposals, Robert F. Kantin. Bob is President of SalesProposals.com and the author of several books including *Sales Proposals Kit for Dummies*. He was kind enough to let us include the following excerpt from one of his recent books.

From *Strategic Proposals: Closing the Big Deal*
by Robert F. Kantin

Sales professionals may do everything right during the sale, but if they don't integrate the development of a strong, strategic proposal into the process, they put their sales at risk.

Strategic Proposal Structure

A strategic proposal contains five main sections. These sections are interrelated and customer-focused. They categorize information and provide a logical sequence of information and ideas.

1. **Background Information** identifies the buyer's current situation, the improvement opportunity, the buyer's unresolved problem or unachieved opportunity, and the basis for the proposal. Some recommended Section 1 subsections include:

   - Industry Background

   - Client/Customer Background

   - Current Operations or Functions

   - Improvement Opportunity [Definition, Analysis, and Plans]

   - Client/Customer Needs and Objectives

   - Purpose of This Proposal

2. **Proposed Business Solution** presents the seller's proposed custom application of their products or services, and details how the seller will help the buyer achieve the improvement opportunity.

   Section 2 of a strategic proposal should contain four recommended subsections:

   - Product or Service Description

   - Product of Service Application

   - Non-financial (Qualitative) Benefits

   - Financial (Quantitative) Benefits

3. **Implementation Management** presents the seller's implementation methodology or project management

practices and schedules to assure the buyer that the seller is able to deliver on the contract.

Like the first two strategic proposal sections that have definite subsection requirements, the third proposal section has three recommended subsections:

- Methods: implementation, project, engagement, or management methods (or practices)

- Team: implementation, project, engagement, or client service team

- Schedule: implementation, project, or engagement schedule

4. **Seller Profile** discusses the seller's qualifications and business practices to further assure the buyer that the seller will be able to deliver on the contract and provide ongoing service.

   This section has six suggested subsections:

   - Mission or Customer Service Philosophy Statement

   - Company or Corporate Overview

   - Quality

   - Customer References

   - Why us?

   - Design and Development Checklist

5. **Business Issues** profiles the seller's business and groups all business-related items for ease of review and reference, such as fees/prices, assumptions used for scheduling and pricing expenses, and when and how the seller will invoice the buyer.

6. [In this **last section**], most sellers will find that three subsections suffice:

   - Assumptions—i.e. to adhere to the implementation schedule, a software development consultant might assume the buyer will review and approve design documents within five business days of receipt.

   - Fees/Prices and Other Expenses

   - Invoicing Schedule

Proposal Components

Additionally, a strategic proposal should include the following components:

- **Title Page**
- **Executive Summary**—as its name implies, a concise synopsis of the entire proposal
- **Table of Contents**—a listing of main sections and subsections with page numbers
- **Appendices**—used to support information contained in the main proposal sections; a place for preprinted form, detailed financial calculations, product specifications, etc.

Use Appendices for Preprinted Materials

The overall appearance of a proposal is ruined when the seller includes preprinted materials in main proposal sections. Preprinted materials will interrupt a proposal's flow of information and ideas. Often when a writer puts a brochure or specifications sheet in the middle of a proposal section, he or she wants the recipient to find critical information in the document. The recipient would be better served if the seller summarized the information in one or two paragraphs and used the preprinted material as a supporting appendix.

Proposal Structure at a Glance

Executive Summary

1. Background Information

    a. Industry Information

    b. Background

    c. Current Operation or Functions

    d. Improvement Opportunity [definition, analysis, and plans]

    e. Needs and Objectives [buyer]

    f. Purpose of this Proposal

2. Proposed Solution

    a. Product or Service Description

    b. Product or Service Application (optional)

    c. Nonfinancial Benefits

    d. Financial Benefits

3. Implementation

   a. *Engagement or Project Management Methods*

   b. *Schedule*

   c. *Team*

4. Seller Profile

   a. *Mission Statement*

   b. *Company Profile*

   c. *Quality*

   d. *Why Us?*

   e. *Other subsections based on seller's industry or profession*

5. Business Issues

   a. *Assumptions*

   b. *Fees/Prices [and other expenses]*

   c. *Invoicing Schedule*

6. Appendices

Our thanks to Bob Kantin for allowing us to include this important material. You can reach Bob at:

SalesProposals.com
2600 Ventura Drive, Suite 13210
Plano, TX 75093
1-972-612-4160
www.salesproposals.com

We asked the Buyers: What percentage of reps provide you with quality proposals?

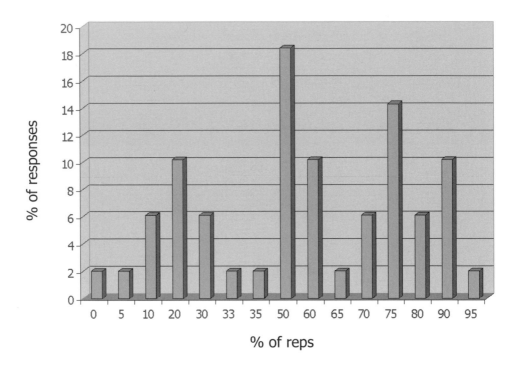

We asked the Buyers: On a scale of 1 to 10, how important is the quality of the sales proposal when you decide if you will give a vendor your business?

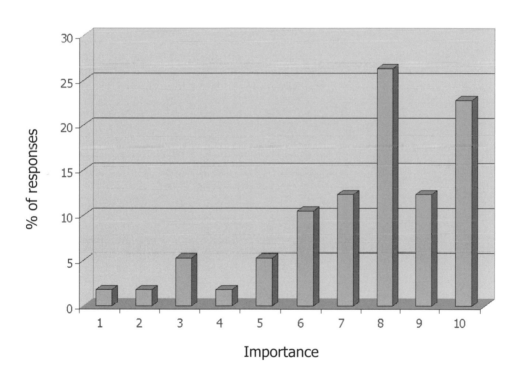

Comments from the Buyers

Kristen Mitchell
Senior Buyer
Boston Financial
Data Services Inc.

"Proposals are very important as they help us create a short list of the top two or three vendors. These vendors get the opportunity to come in and do a formal presentation."

Greg Tennyson,
C.P.M., CPCM
Vice President,
Corporate Procurement
Oracle Corporation:

"The proposal is very important—a nine or ten out of ten. The proposal provides an opportunity for sales reps' to do their homework, demonstrate their knowledge, and clearly articulate their value proposition to our buying group."

Peggy Jones
Operations/H.R. Director
Magic Software Enterprises,
Inc.

"Proposals are very important, and most of the ones I receive are well done. A comprehensive proposal is a good way to demonstrate that you've done your homework."

Kenneth F. Esbin
Purchasing Manager
Tarmac America

"A good proposal tells me a great deal about the company's professionalism. If they have a professional presentation, it tells me they care about their company's perception in the marketplace."

Larry Stanley
Senior Supply Chain
Analyst

"In terms of importance, this is definitely a ten out of ten. At our company, an incomplete proposal won't even be considered."

Krysia Diaz, CEBS
Benefits Supervisor

"Approximately 50 percent of the proposals I receive are high-quality. We recently received a couple that were really, really well done. They did an excellent job in giving us the exact information we wanted. When you get that kind of response, it makes it that much easier for you to lean to one side or the other. When you're dealing with two vendors and haven't decided which one to choose, extra effort in this area may tip the scales in the favor of one vendor."

Closing

5

Tip 1

When you ask for the order, keep it simple and direct

There are many well-known closing methods in the sales business. You've probably heard of some of these:

- The Red Herring Close
- The Secondary Question Close
- The Sharp Angle Close
- The Lost Sale Close
- The Affirmative No Close
- The Similar Situation Close
- The Buying Criteria Close
- The Assumptive Close
- The Ben Franklin Close
- The Value-Added Close
- The Instant Reverse Close
- The Change-Places Close

If you've followed the steps we've explained so far, you shouldn't have to resort to such elaborate closers. Closing should be a seamless process—simple and direct:

Sales Rep: "I'd like to go ahead and book this order. Does that work for you?"

In the course of our research, we submitted the following closing questions to the buyers and asked for their comments:

A. We can arrange delivery for the 15th, no problem. Is there anything else you need to know to move ahead with this order?

B. If we can arrange delivery on the 15th, can you think of any reason why we shouldn't set it up now?

C. Let's arrange for delivery on the 15th, is that okay?

71 percent of the buyers preferred question A—provided by Art Sobczak, President of Business By Phone Inc. *(see pg. 52)*. The buyers' comments appear on the next page.

Comments from the Buyers

Jason Wihnon
Supply Purchaser
IKON–IMS

"Question A is an eight out of ten. It tells the customer that the rep has everything in place for the sale to go through providing nothing else is required. It's direct but not overly pushy."

Roy Sekigawa
Purchasing Operations Manager
Foremost Dairies, Hawaii

"Question A gets an eight out of ten. It shows that the seller actually wants the best for the buyer by asking if additional info is required to meet the buyer's complete satisfaction."

Robert Romero, CPIM
Supply Chain Manager
Superior Communications

"Question A deserves seven out of ten. It is more considerate, sincere, and makes it seem as though you really are interested in taking care of the customer."

Kathi Wilson
Facilities Assistant
IDX Systems Corporation

"Question A rates ten out of ten. It illustrates that you can provide the service on the terms the buyer needs, and the open-ended question allows communication. It's informal, flows well and it's not pushy."

Anonymous

"I like Question A and rate it an eight out of ten because it's asking me if we need anything further, and they've already said they can make arrangements to deliver when I need it."

Lisa Perdue
Senior Buyer

"Question A is nine out of ten. It sounds more professional, more customer service-oriented. Question B sounds a little pushy."

Anonymous

"Question A gets ten out of ten. I don't like the pressure of the other two. A is direct, it is specific, and he's asking if there's anything else he can do for us."

Lupe Rodriguez
Facilities Coordinator

"Question A is my favorite and I rate it seven out of ten. Asking if there's anything else you need to know is a good idea. The more information that's confirmed at the end of a conversation the better; that way nothing is forgotten and there are no mistakes."

Phyllis Pierce

Purchasing / Accounts Receivable Manager

"I give Question A ten out of ten. It is more subtle than the other two questions. I like the fact that it asks the buyer if there is anything more that the selling company can do."

Maintaining

6

Tip 1   At appropriate intervals, send your customers a
          brief email to check on their satisfaction

Tip 2   Stay in touch with your customers by providing
          them with useful information and resources

With most sales reps, there is not enough follow-up after the sale. Service after the sale is just as important as service before the sale. Buyers want to know that the people they are dealing with, and investing their money and time in, are going to be around for the long term.

—Trent N. Baker, C.P.M., Purchasing Manager
Wilson Foods, Division of Reser's Fine Foods, Inc.

At appropriate intervals, send your customers a brief email to check on their satisfaction

It takes a lot of time and effort to acquire a customer, so it makes sense to be proactive about ensuring their complete satisfaction. If you ask, a customer may tell you there's a problem—but if you don't, they may just take their business elsewhere. By sending a brief email at appropriate intervals, you let your customer know they are valued, and you may get the chance to nip any problems in the bud.

(See example, next page)

Example: Follow-up message

We asked the Buyers: What percentage of sales reps contact you after the sale to make sure everything went well, and to ensure your ongoing satisfaction?

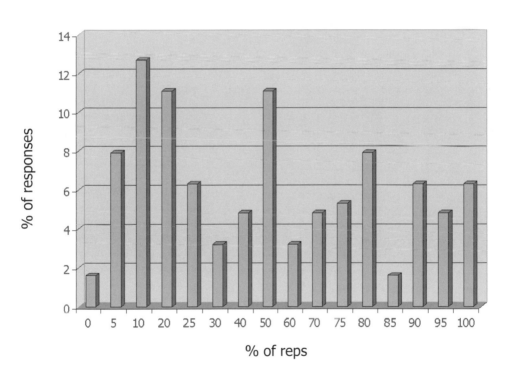

We asked the Buyers: On a scale of 1 to 10, how important is this to you?

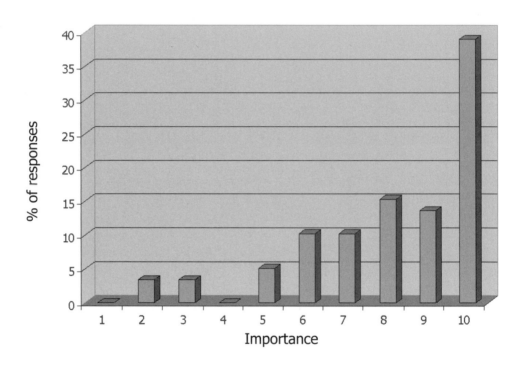

Comments from the Buyers

**Charles Tobler,
C.P.M., MPP**
Senior Buyer

"Many times a salesperson has made an impression on me and I've bought from him. But the next time I needed the product, I couldn't remember the names of the rep or company. Why? Because I never heard from them again after the sale. You must maintain your name and product recognition with the buyer."

Thea Bremer
Buyer

"This type of survey would tell me that they are truly interested in doing business with me and providing me with the best service that they can."

Cathy Cooper
*Vice President,
Marketing Manager
Washington Federal Savings*

"Another post-sale problem is when companies have turnover among their reps and the company doesn't bother to assign somebody for continued follow-up. I dislike having to track down a sales manager to figure out how to buy from their company again. New reps should demand prior sales records so they can follow up with the clients of the reps they replace."

I value service and communication above all else. It would be helpful if sales reps could present new and innovative ideas and share any relevant information.

—Hillary Berk, Group Manager of Marketing, Supply Chain
Elizabeth Arden

Stay in touch with your customers by providing them with useful information and resources

It's important to follow up with customers, but buyers are busy people; they simply don't have time for phone calls and visits without a specific purpose. How can you maintain contact with them without being annoying?

One way is to give your customers value-added information and resources. This is a good way to build strong business relationships and customer loyalty.

Examples: Following Up by Adding Value

Here are some ways you can follow up with your customers by offering them extra value:

- Forward your customers noteworthy articles or information relevant to their industry.

- Provide your customers with referrals.

- Conduct objective information-based seminars *(see pg. 23)*.

Comments from the Buyers

Kristen Mitchell
Senior Buyer,
Boston Financial
Data Services Incorporated

"My office-supply vendor once brought together different manufacturers that they deal with and hosted a session about products that were of potential value to us."

Bruce R. Weener
Vice President,
Customer Satisfaction
American Seating Company

"Training definitely adds value to the relationship after the sale in terms of technology, new materials, and new processes. I like to be kept informed. Communicate, communicate, communicate."

Wm. Frank Quiett,
C.P.M., A.P.P.
Project Lead
Supply Chain Management
and Strategic Sourcing

"The most effective thing a sales rep can do for me after the sale is to follow up with confirmation on activities associated with the sale, without being asked! If I have to ask, that is not customer satisfaction—that is customer-problem resolution. If the action comes before the customer has to ask, that is proactive team building and the beginning of a collaborative relationship."

Greg Tennyson,
C.P.M., CPCM
Vice President
Corporate Procurement
Oracle Corporation

"[The supplier] could step back and look at relevant business processes to see how we can re-engineer them together to be more efficient and effective. The supplier could then meet with us to explore areas where they might be able to provide some cost savings."

Richard K. Tyler, C.P.M.
Director of Purchasing
MRC Bearings

"I consider sales reps the experts in their respective areas. As such, I expect them to come to me continually with ways to reduce cost and improve value."

Communicating

7

Tip 1   Keep your promises: Commit to a target date and confirm completion

Tip 2   Prepare and rehearse important voice mail messages in advance

Tip 3a   Record role-plays to improve your communication skills

Tip 3b   Identify weak words and phrases and eliminate them from your business vocabulary

Tip 4   Provide your customer with a knowledgeable and informed backup person to contact when you are absent

Tip 5   Following your sales meeting, email the buyer a summary of the key points you discussed

Follow-up is tremendously important and an email would be fine. I'll give you an example of what happens more often than not: I'll ask for a usage history or some other documentation, and they'll pass it on to their administrative staff. Then they walk in the next month and say, "So what can we do for you?" I'll say, "I'm still waiting for that usage report from last month," and he'll say, "What do you mean? I told my office to take care of that." Why didn't he take ownership and follow up for me with his own company?

—Kenneth F. Esbin, Purchasing Manager
Tarmac America

Keep your promises: Commit to a target date and confirm completion

Dependability is a valued commodity in business—yet buyers tell us it is not uncommon for busy sales reps to make promises they don't keep.

The problem is time. There is never enough—and an unscheduled item on your to-do list routinely gets bumped by items that do have target dates. By committing to a target date, promises become practical and you become accountable.

Depending on the situation, the next step would be to confirm completion of the task/promise/commitment via email or with a short voice mail message.

We asked the Buyers: On a scale of 0 to 10, how useful is it when a rep makes a brief follow-up call or emails you to confirm the fulfillment of a promise?

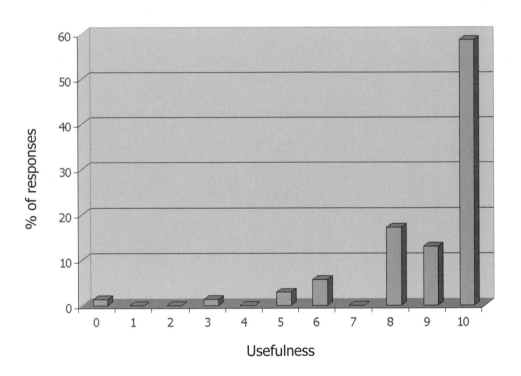

We asked the Buyers: What percentage of reps actually do this each time?

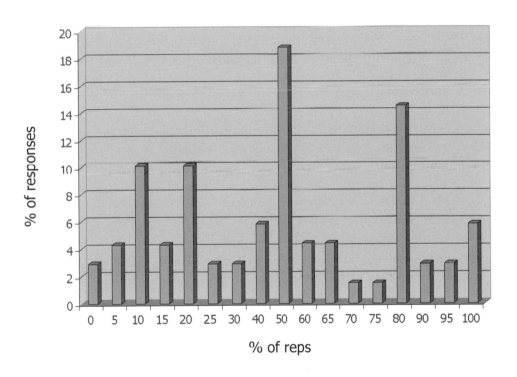

Comments from the Buyers

Greg Graham
Buyer
Kenworth Truck Company

"I like this approach. It suggests they are competent professionals who follow through, and that raises my comfort level."

David Frieder
Purchasing Director
Planet Automotive
Group Inc.

"Only about 20 percent of the reps I've dealt with are true pros who always follow up to ensure the whole job is done—and done right."

Anonymous

"If a sales rep cannot keep a commitment, I would rather hear the truth instead of excuses. As a buyer, I have to communicate the status of various components to our entire internal group (manufacturing, production, etc). If you rely on a commitment made by the seller, and the commitment turns out to be false, the buyer is the one who takes all the blame."

Alan B. Rifkin
Senior Buyer

"I would like to hear from reps, so that I can pass on the information to the people in my company who need to know the promised transaction has been completed. It helps keep me on top of things. I deal with several reps who don't always follow through on promises and I find that extremely annoying."

Andrew Jules DeGiulio
Purchasing Manager

"Accountability is essential to the business transaction. It flows both ways as does respect. A sales person who sets a realistic target date and confirms completion earns my respect and therefore the privilege to expand the business relationship."

I won't return messages that are not decipherable, use poor grammar, or make no real point. You have only one opportunity to get it right, so rehearse the call, and make sure that what you say has substance. Once you leave the message, you can't take it back.

—Errol van Edema, Manager of Purchasing & Manufacturing/Distribution

Tip 2

Prepare and rehearse important voice mail messages in advance

Considering the importance of voice mail, there is a real lack of guidance in the art of leaving effective messages.

How often have you had to play a voice mail message several times because you could not understand the caller's name or phone number? And how many rambling and unplanned messages have you had to endure? How can you avoid this pitfall with your own voice mail messages?

Here are some key steps to ensure clarity and professionalism:

1. **Plan and prepare.** Before you make the call, assume the prospect will be busy and that you will have to leave a message. Script out the essential points of your message.

2. **Rehearse or role-play.** A quick run run-through helps ensure your message will be communicated clearly and concisely.

3. **Start *and* end the message with your number.** Begin and end your message by clearly stating your name, company name, and phone number.

We asked the Buyers: What percentage of reps' voice mail messages are difficult to understand, missing key information, or must be played several times to identify the name or phone number?

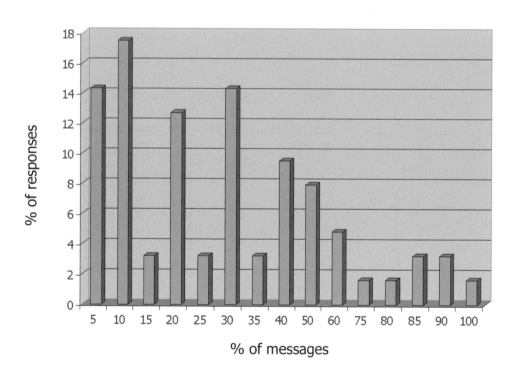

We asked the Buyers: On a scale of 0 to 10, how important
are effective voice mail messages to
you?

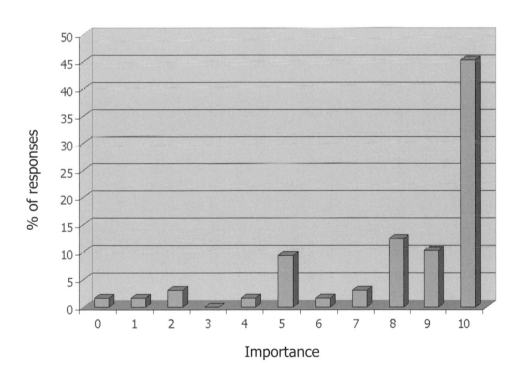

Comments from the Buyers

Beckie Beard,
C.P.M, A.P.P, CACM
Director, Purchasing &
Materials Management
Lansing Community College

"Many sales reps do not rehearse what they are going to say, or they speak way too fast. Keep messages short and sweet, and leave a phone number only if it is a local or toll-free call. Don't ask customers to return your call long-distance!"

Lou Riley
Senior Director
Materials Management

"I think that messages should be clear and to the point. I receive many calls throughout the day and I don't have time to listen to someone go on and on."

Judy Elrite, C.P.M.
Buyer Specialist

"Most reps say the phone number so fast that it takes three listens to get it. If the message is poorly delivered, I won't return the call. My job is phone-intensive and I'm very busy."

Tip 3a

Record role-plays to improve your communication skills

Recording role-plays with a colleague can help improve your ability to communicate effectively and intelligently. By taping your self, you may discover communication habits you were unaware of and could improve. During our re-search, we found that very few reps do this—yet those who did reported dramatic improvements in their confidence and communication skills. As a result, they made more appointments and closed more sales.

Clearly, it's important to make a positive impression when speaking with prospects and customers. When you listen to your tape, check for these problems:

- Are you speaking too quickly?
- Do you sound unconfident?
- Do you speak in a monotone?
- Could you sound more sincere?
- Are you talking over the other person, or interrupting?
- Could you use more inflection to convey energy and impact where required?

Tip 3b

Identify weak words and phrases and eliminate them from your business vocabulary

Using your taped role-plays *(see pg. 123)*, identify and work on eliminating weak, indecisive phrases and words such as:

- "Do you know what I mean?"
- "To tell you the truth…"
- "To be honest with you…"
- "I guess"
- "I hope"
- "I think"
- "Maybe"
- "Sort of"
- "Kind of"
- "Probably"
- "Possibly"
- "Basically"
- "Hopefully"

Planning Guide:

Replacing Weak Words

Write down some of the weak words you tend to use and would like to remove from your business vocabulary:

_____

_____

_____

_____

_____

_____

_____

Having a back up contact is very helpful, I would rate this 8 out of 10. It saves time, and keeps communication between our companies open and accessible.

—Brian Moran, Director Americas, Supply Management
Siemens Westinghouse Power Corporation

Provide your customer with a knowledgeable and informed backup person to contact when you are absent

When a customer needs a quick answer and you're not available, should they have to wait while your staff looks for information only you have access to? No. Make it a priority to introduce all of your clients to someone at your company who can cover for you when you can't be there.

You can introduce your backup with a three-way call, or simply give the buyer your backup's business card. Be sure your backup can access and fully understand all of your relevant account information so they can fill in for you effectively.

Comments from the Buyers

Leslie Champion
*Senior Procurement
Specialist
Industrial Design &
Construction, Inc.*

"I find it quite helpful to have a backup contact when I need information. Nothing is more annoying than not being able to get answers when you need them."

**Anthony Natali,
C.P.M., A.P.P.**
*National Purchasing
Manager*

"The lack of a knowledgeable backup contact is extremely irritating. A person who answers the phone in the customer service department should not be considered a backup."

Lori Patten
*Director of Projects–
Development
Hyatt Hotels Corporation*

"Most reps don't provide a regular back up contact, but it would definitely be helpful. It's frustrating having to spend so much time sifting through company voice-mail directories trying to find someone to answer my question when my sales rep is not available."

Tina M. Lowenthal
*Associate Director,
Purchasing Services
California Institute
of Technology*

"Providing a backup person is an effective way for sales reps to provide better service. One of our large suppliers always has backup contacts in place and since we work closely together, it makes for a great working relationship. It's much easier to work with them."

An email summary would be very helpful; it's always good to have written clarification of key points. It shows they're paying attention and that they're on top of things. In five years, perhaps two percent of the reps I've met with have ever emailed a written summary of key points after a meeting.

—Kristen Mitchell, Senior Buyer
Boston Financial Data Services Inc.

Tip 5

Following your sales meeting, email the buyer a summary of the key points you discussed

Don't necessarily limit your email summaries to follow-ups of meetings. An email summary of key points discussed in a telephone call is a great way to ensure effective communication and accountability, and provides an opportunity for the other party to add any points of their own.

Here is an example of an email message summarizing a meeting:

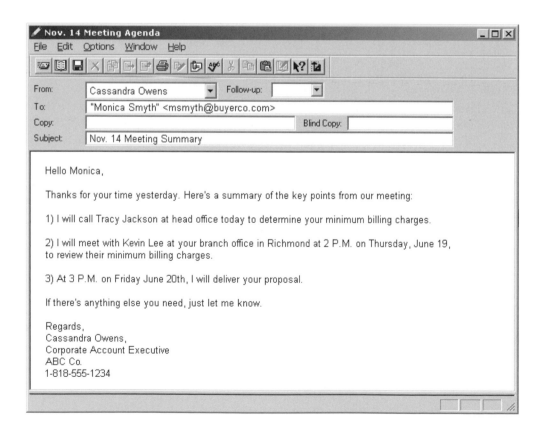

Nov. 14 Meeting Agenda

File   Edit   Options   Window   Help

From: Cassandra Owens   Follow-up:
To: "Monica Smyth" <msmyth@buyerco.com>
Copy: Blind Copy:
Subject: Nov. 14 Meeting Summary

Hello Monica,

Thanks for your time yesterday. Here's a summary of the key points from our meeting:

1) I will call Tracy Jackson at head office today to determine your minimum billing charges.

2) I will meet with Kevin Lee at your branch office in Richmond at 2 P.M. on Thursday, June 19, to review their minimum billing charges.

3) At 3 P.M. on Friday June 20th, I will deliver your proposal.

If there's anything else you need, just let me know.

Regards,
Cassandra Owens,
Corporate Account Executive
ABC Co.
1-818-555-1234

Comments from the Buyers

Jeffrey J. Dodig
National Accounts Mgr.
Forest City Residential

"I think emailing a summary after the first meeting is important, because I don't want to do business with the guy who's just trying to make a quick sale and isn't interested in following up—and I never hear from him again."

Dean R. Schlosser, Jr.
Purchasing Agent

"An email summary would be very helpful. I always take notes at meetings and it would be helpful to compare the rep's summary with mine."

Chris Nield
Corporate Buyer
International Truck
and Engine Corp.

"It's very important, especially for buyers that don't have meeting minutes. I usually have meeting minutes, which I usually send to all involved. So an email summary and minutes for comparison would be very helpful."

Hillary Berk
Group Manager of
Marketing, Supply Chain
Elizabeth Arden

"It's called follow-up, and after working twelve hours it's helpful to have a reminder!"

Ken Fuqua
Purchasing Administrator

"I find this very useful since it allows me to start an email file to keep track of my relationship with the vendor."

Krysia Diaz, CEBS
Benefits Supervisor

"That would be great—very helpful, because many times we put stuff aside when we are busy with all the things going on in our department. When we get the email, it's nice to have that to refer to."

Randy Shepherd
Systems Coordinator,
Senior Buyer

"I always ask for a follow-up email from the rep after the meeting to help me communicate with my colleagues and keep everything organized and filed."

We asked the Buyers: Assuming a rep verbally summarized the key points of your first meeting, how helpful is it, on a scale of 1 to 10, when the rep also emails you the summary the next day?

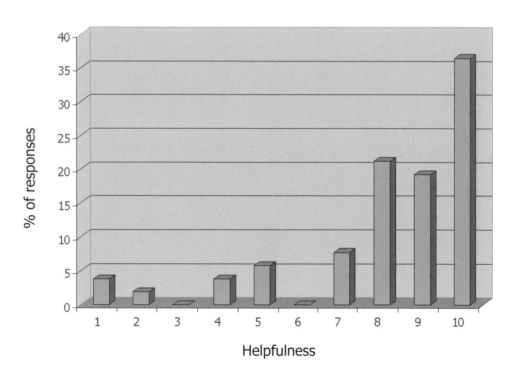

We asked the Buyers: What percentage of reps actually present and email you these summaries?

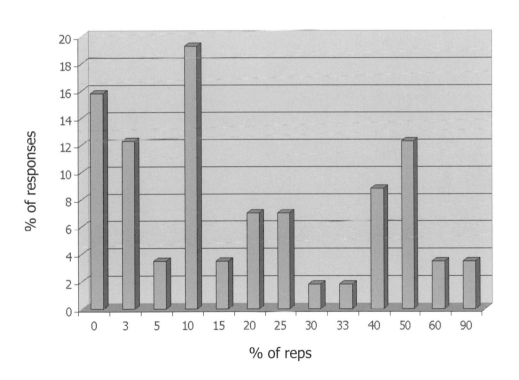

Annoying

8

Tip 1

How to annoy buyers—guaranteed

When it comes to creating and keeping customers, it's also important to know what *not* to do.

We asked the buyers to tell us about some annoying things sales reps do. We have placed their responses into the following categories:

- Being unprepared for meetings
- Overpromising and underdelivering
- Back-door selling
- Being insincere or concealing information
- Continuously cold-calling or showing up without an appointment
- Being too persistent or aggressive
- Talking too much; showing poor listening skills
- Failing to do post-sale follow-up

Comments from the Buyers

Being unprepared for meetings

Michael Tator

*V.P., Director of Production
Wunderman, of the Y&R
Companies, Irvine*

- Being unprepared with their information or material
- Showing up late for meetings
- Not telling me that they are bringing additional people to the meeting beforehand
- Not having the proper equipment for making the presentation
- Dragging the meeting out too long

Judy Elrite, C.P.M.

Buyer Specialist

"It's annoying when reps haven't done their research on my company. I also don't like it when they ask me who the 'other' supplier is. They should know who the competition is in my area."

Christopher Locke

*Global Lead Buyer
DaimlerChrysler Corp.*

"It's frustrating when sales reps do not understand our specifications and requirements. They assume they know how we want our equipment built based on prior programs and do not even read the current specs.

"Another source of frustration is that the quote packages they send us clearly show their inability to comprehend what we're asking for. Even the simplest of requests are wrong. For example, I usually ask for three quote packages: two unpriced and one priced. You can't believe the variations I get: two priced and one unpriced; three priced, three unpriced; one unpriced and one priced."

Anne Stilwell

*Director, Contract and
Procurement Services
Fannie Mae*

"I'm not impressed when reps meet with me without doing research on our company. Instead, they use up half of the meeting time asking me for basic information. If they were true professionals, they would have done this before they came to see me. It's also annoying when they fail to plan the meeting so that the important content is covered in the time allocated.

"It is also irritating when reps show up at follow-up meetings without having answers to questions that were asked at the initial meeting."

**Greg Tennyson,
C.P.M., CPCM**

*Vice President,
Corporate Procurement
Oracle Corporation*

"Coming in and giving a cold pitch and not having done their homework is probably the most annoying thing, because it's a waste of my time and theirs. "

**Lawrence K. Buker,
C.P.M., CPIM**

*Corporate Purchasing /
Travel Manager, QAD Inc.*

"It's annoying when I get a call and the rep asks, 'What does your company do?' The first thing I think is: This guy hasn't even gone to our website, or he doesn't even know who he's calling, and I'm not going to take the time to explain. Reps should already know that before they knock on the door."

Overpromising and underdelivering

Karen Gyarfas-Lavallee

*Studio Manager–Director of
Print Production
Landor Associates, of the
Y&R Companies, Irvine*

"I get annoyed by things like sloppy follow-up, being late for appointments, and not respecting my time."

Anonymous

"Promising things that they are not able to do and price changes without notification are both very annoying."

Vivian Green

Production Manager
Wunderman, of the
Y&R Companies, Irvine

"I find it annoying when reps are forgetful—usually because they didn't take notes—or are slow to follow through on delivering information I've requested."

Jason Wihnon

Supply Purchaser
IKON–IMS

"It's annoying when they break procedures that are already in place just to close the sale, and then they end up not delivering on the promise. Just be up-front and promise what you can deliver. Missing deadlines is terrible. Don't say you can do something knowing you won't be able to."

"Back-door" Selling

Chuck Stanasek, C.P.M.

Materials Manager

"An annoying things is 'back-door' selling—bypassing the procurement group and dealing directly with the various departments, such as Engineering."

Fred Wilson

Procurement Manager–
Industrial Engineer

"I know one thing that really ticks off buyers: going over their head or around through the back door. That just doesn't sit very well with me. From that moment on, I'm open to the idea of someone replacing him."

Toni Horn, C.P.M.

Global Commodity Mgr.
Silicon Graphics Inc.

"It annoys me when reps attempt to rework their way into the company and pitch their products and services to others outside the purchasing department, after we've told them 'No'."

Kathi Wilson

Facilities Assistant
IDX Systems Corporation

"I find it frustrating when I have rejected their proposal, and they call back at another time attempting to speak to another buyer. It's unethical and sneaky, and it makes for bad business."

Lawrence K. Buker,
C.P.M., CPIM

Corporate Purchasing /
Travel Manager
QAD Inc.

"It's annoying when they follow up and I say, 'We're going to have to get back to you,' or 'There's been a delay,' and they start talking to other people in the company to try and advance the sale. This can annoy a buyer so much that the next time an opportunity comes, we don't call them."

Being insincere or concealing information

Linda J. Mahran
Manager,
Non-Product Purchasing

"One serious annoyance is when the seller calls and doesn't identify what product or service they are offering. Not being up-front is not the way to handle a sales call."

Robert Romero, CPIM
Supply Chain Manager
Superior Communications

"Some of the things that annoy me are the sales reps who come across a little too sweet, a little too nice, to the point where you see it's not sincere; it's just a little too sugar-coated. I prefer someone who is more down to earth, truthful and genuine."

Continuously cold-calling or showing up without an appointment

Lisa Perdue
Senior Buyer

"Some reps just keep calling and calling. If I don't call back, it's because I don't need their service, or I'm not interested. Constantly calling me and annoying me is going to push me off even farther."

Sharon Spear
Production Manager
Wunderman, of the
Y&R Companies, Irvine

"I find it very annoying when reps drop by without an appointment."

Stan Marshall, C.P.M.
Purchasing Manager

"It bothers me when they visit with no appointment. I hate it when they just show up. This will never land them a sale with me."

Sheryl Haeberle
Buyer
Brigham Young University,
Idaho

"I dislike it when reps just show up with out letting me know they are coming. My time is valuable. I often stop buying from repeat offenders."

Christopher Locke
Global Lead Buyer
DaimlerChrysler Corp.

"Suppliers who show up unannounced at the buyer's desk and expect a major dialog really frustrate me. For every telephone call, email, and meeting one supplier sets up with the buyer, there are at least a dozen more suppliers calling, emailing, and expecting time for discussion."

Being too persistent or aggressive

Charles B. Detrick, C.P.M
Purchasing Manager
Harris Automation

"Overcalling. Reps are always calling, even when I've left a message to tell them that I will get back to them Sometimes I need to put the rep off because I have to wait for people to get back to me first, so I don't have an answer for a rep at that time, but some keep calling anyway."

James L. Semala
Buyer/Planner, NISource

"It's annoying when you get an overabundance of follow up calls from reps to find out if the successful bidder has been chosen. When you have 15 people calling you 15 times each to ask when the decision will be made, it gets frustrating."

Lorna Good
Senior Production Manager
Wunderman, of the
Y&R Companies, Irvine

"Calling too often! Some reps call to inquire about the status of projects every single day, even after they have been told that they will be contacted if they are awarded the job. I have told these same reps that I am extremely busy and do not have time to call them back, or even listen to unnecessary voice mails, but they keep calling."

Linda J. Mahran
Manager,
Non-Product Purchasing

"Continuing to sell after I have said that I am not interested is not the way to do business. A little persistence is okay, but going overboard is not."

Cliffton Durham
Product Manager

"Being far too persistent when I'm not interested. In the future, even if this rep has an item that we might need, I would not be inclined to do business with them."

Talking too much; showing poor listening skills

Richard K. Tyler, C.P.M. *Director of Purchasing* *MRC Bearings*	"It's annoying when reps don't listen! Some reps push, push, push, and just want to close the sale. You can't shove yourself down someone's throat."
Trent N. Baker, C.P.M. *Purchasing Manager* *Wilson Foods, Division of* *Reser's Fine Foods, Inc.*	"I get annoyed when reps spend most of the time talking about themselves or their company without listening to me and trying to understand my needs and about my company."
David Mizer *Vice President* *Strategic Sourcing* *Carnival Cruise Lines Inc.*	"The biggest thing that annoys me about reps is that they don't listen. You can have a meeting with a rep and explain what your parameters are in business, what your limitations are, what your decision process is and why, maybe at that time, their service is not something that you can pursue. But some of them don't hear you. They continue to push and push, and that's very irritating. The problem is that it really puts that sales rep in a negative position for any and all future contact for business, because you don't want to have to deal with an aggressive salesperson."
Roy Sekigawa *Purchasing* *Operations Manager* *Foremost Dairies, Hawaii*	"It's annoying when reps assume what the buyers needs are before asking. Too much talk, not enough questions."

Failing to do post-sale follow-up

David Frieder *Purchasing Director* *Planet Automotive Group* *Inc.*	"It's annoying when reps make promises they cannot keep to get the account. Too often the rep gets the initial order, then forgets about us."
Anonymous	"Servicing the sale, after the contract is signed, is often ignored—yet that's when service has to be at its best, to keep the new customer."

Jeffrey J. Dodig
National Accounts Manager
ForestCity Residential

"I dislike reps who make the sale—and then that's it. When you have questions or you need help, or your users need to be trained, all of a sudden they're very difficult to get hold of. When I need to buy some products, they're there to sell them. When I need some follow-up work, or responses, or help with issues that aren't related to sales, I want to know they're going to be there."

Buyer Contributions

Greg Adkins Purchasing Manager
20

Lori Aljets Purchasing and Quality Assurance Manager
Norpac Foods Inc.
54, 63

Trent N. Baker, C.P.M. Purchasing Manager
Wilson Foods, Division of Reser's Fine Foods, Inc.
54, 105, 140

Scott Bartel Sourcing Strategist
54

Beckie Beard, C.P.M, A.P.P, CACM Director, Purchasing & Materials Management
Lansing Community College
40, 122

Hillary Berk Group Manager of Marketing, Supply Chain
Elizabeth Arden
110, 129

Brad Bigelow Manager of Purchasing and Vendor Relations
31

Thea Bremer Buyer
109

Lawrence K. Buker, C.P.M., CPIM Corporate Purchasing/Travel Manager
QAD Inc.
136, 137

Leslie Champion Senior Procurement Specialist
Industrial Design & Construction, Inc.
59, 127

Robert Click Purchasing Manager
26

Carl Colasurdo Director of Purchasing
20, 82

Cathy Cooper Vice President, Marketing Manager
Washington Federal Savings
109

Index

ABOUT THE AUTHOR

Michael Schell is founder and president of the Marketshare Group of Companies in Vancouver, British Columbia:

Marketshare Communications Inc.

Marketshare Publications Inc.

Marketshare Corporate Sales Training Inc.

A respected teacher of sales and customer-service skills with more than 20 years of corporate experience, Michael has often thought: *If you're going to write a book, write the one you always wanted to read but could never find.* This is that book.

For information about Marketshare services and programs, call toll-free at **1-877-870-0009** or visit Marketshare's website at **www.marketshareinc.com**